VOICES OF THUNDER

New Work
From the Institute of American Indian Arts

Editors

Heather Ahtone
Chris Apache
Neilwood R. Begay
Sorrel Goodwin
Allison Hedge Coke
Christian Pappan
Melissa Pope
Maxine Smith
Rose Spahan
Carlson Vicenti

IAIA Anthology Series:

New Work, 1989
Desire and Time, 1990
Masked Spirits, 1991

For information:
Creative Writing Program
Institute of American Indian Arts Press
P.O. Box 20007
Santa Fe, NM 87504

ISBN: 1-881396-03-7

CONTRIBUTORS

APOTHEOSIS
Heather Ahtone

Words oozing and caressing and shaping my brain
Volcanic eruption sending fire into the sky
Heat penetrates my body
My blood is boiling and I am scared
Rush and flow through my veins
Head booming like a bass drum in an orchestra
Creation force driving nails in my hands
Sucking my artery to taste cherry flavoring
Restraint is my own

Go ahead and envelope me
Send me to a different place
Not new or exciting
A place filled with concrete and steel
With bloodless veins and corroded pipes rusted from the air
   that I breathe
Go ahead and manipulate me
Change my field of vision
Taking away the jasmine and peacocks and Santa Fe sunsets
Replace them with test patterns and bad sitcoms
Masking my energy with electricity
Inject me with saccharine and nicotine
I will smile and laugh
I will fill your space with nonentities to convince you that I
   know nothing
Go ahead and sabotage me
Escorting me though minefields
Pushing me on with your words of encouragement
Helping me to find hidden pitfalls I might miss on my own
You convince me that I am at fault so that I commit suicide
   and save you the trouble of annihilating my children

I see what you are doing
Your plan to erase my voice from a planet you burn for
　　pleasure
Fill my head with your three faced god of eternal damnation
　　who died on the cross for you
Chain me to your confusion and throw me in a river filled
　　with carnivorous subtleties
Believe your treatise of sacrament and superstition
Confess your sins to your god of forgiveness while you roll
　　and smoke the world he created for you
Addict yourselves to the euphoria of destruction
I watch in horror as you drain your cup of human blood and
　　wipe the guilt away with the back of your martyred hand

Your genocide will end when you realize you have massacred
　　the last of the living
You will be left standing in a desert covered with scattered
　　bones drying from mushroom clouded heat
In the distance you will see a mirage
The utopia you had envisioned in your stupor will draw
　　you forward
Pulling you over the children whose bones lie against the
　　skeleton called Mother
Grabbing your hair and dragging you through the rubble
　　called Home
Filling your mind with technicolor abstractions of a new
　　beginning
Filling your bones with a lust for a higher conscience
You will not resist the omnipotent power which fills the
　　crevices of your brain and muscle tissue
You will welcome with outstretched arms the grace which is
　　befalling you
Screaming praises as you worship the new god you have
　　created

6

(no stanza break)

It will smile and suck your face from your toes to kiss you
    goodnight
You weep from joy and the wetness will begin to burn
Your skin is breaking apart
Your bones are exposed
You crumble into the dust of your ancestors
You have found the face of the beast and it is beautiful

JEN: 人

Heather Ahtone

dark attic haunted
shadows move in rapid motion
searching for serenity
groping for answer in coin toss
divination text says:
"fellowship with man brings deliverance"
relief sought unchallenged by human logic
serendipity   synchronicity
clinging to bending axis
as light reaches doorway
do not enter
darkness shrinks away from
answer found in book
breathing for centuries
guarded by dust in corner of closet
protected by ignorance
unfailing blindness which leads return
trip in a moment to fall on face
bruising hindsight
as hand reaches
throwing fate to the floor

OPHELIA'S RABID SATYR

Heather Ahtone

I watch the candle wax slide down the side of my face
Flame scorches the memories
Until only a puddle is left to be discarded in the morning
I see your smile and your kisses burning slowly
Rising to the ceiling of my hair leaving traces of toxic
    damage
I open the window breathing pungent bitterness
Raging honesty repressed by fragile glass whips coal streaks
    across my face
My eyes close against a bright glare reflected from your gold
    plated alibi
I brace myself for an onslaught commanded by past
    degradations
I clutch at the curtains, my finger bleeds from the thorn on
    the rose pattern bought for my last birthday
Knees buckle under the weight of diamonds impaled on my
    ear lobe
My fall is broken by the chaise upon which you often
    devoured me
I catch my last breath and balance on the edge of insanity
Foot slips   Falling   Falling
To razor sharp rocks, slicing through the facade you created
Standing naked I see clearly through blinding infidelity
I climb the face of your whorishness, stepping in the cracks
    made by your lies
The hands of your mistress hold me steady as I stumble on
    the vows given for my affections
On the summit of my return, I see you in the distance
Brushing my hair
Kissing my back
Licking my ear
I shrug off the uncertainties, smile and recline on the chaise
I lean over to feel the warmth of the flame lighted in your
    memory
And blow.

SILENCE

Heather Ahtone

silence
not the word the
emptiness
filling your gut with a lack a
coldness
of ice crawling on your back through
darkness
clouding your eyes your
surroundings become vague closets of black cloth
covering your fingers your
touch

10

The work in **VOICES OF THUNDER** was solicited, selected, edited, designed, typeset, proofread, corrected, and finalized by : Heather Ahtone, Chris Apache, Neilwood Begay, Sorrel Goodwin, Allison Hedge Coke, Chris Pappan, Melissa Pope, Maxine Smith, Rose Spahan, and Carlson Vicenti as part of Creative Writing 304, Student Anthology class between January 17 -- March 6, 1992. 1300 copies have been printed by McNaughton & Gunn. Thanks to John Garrigan for design assistance.

PLUIE

Philippe Alexandre

It was sublime, stupendous in invention
Who planned the miracles of earth and sky,
Wondrous the power that charged
Small things with secret beauty;
Long branches twining
Green leaves clustering and all
A glimmer, a mist that gently lies
Across the morning sun,
All spangled, darted with fire
Like a starry sky upon the Ancient Tree

The bark of my desiccated skin rests in fiery shadows

I awaken morning from its darkness,
Dress it up with day,
Throw the sash across its chest,
From a passing cloud, or a shawl woven by the sun,
From revolving winds pushed
By the promise that in this vast expanse
There is an aqueous reclining place.
Jadeness settles in the boughs when
An abundance of forces preponderate
Over my parched, foundering roots.

As if the rainbow drinks the clouds,
And drop by drop melts in rain
And children babble under vine trellises,
And the song of rain tickles
The silence of birds on the Tree
Pluie,
Pluie
Pluie

Morning yawns, and the clouds
Pour down their heavy tears,
It rained and rained and rained;
The lake rose above the Treetop,
Suspended.

PETALS OF STONE

Philippe Alexandre

I am one who patiently with a feather's stroke
Brushes the silt from graves in shallow caves
The dead make diagrams in dust among a magical debris
Luck and unlucky stones
A feather finds a goddess in a nest of fingerbones
Her belly and round breasts held as promises

In the hollow mountain shaping water moves under rough
   arch
I follow water-webs thin streams that widen to a pool
And silent on its surface ride rafts of stone petals
In a lightless room a place come close to sleep
An inner dreamland where alterations of the known
Sly shift of elements tangle the sense
An underworld of obsidian lilies

I learn to tell the hours of stone and water
As they move and stay in constancy of change
Water gathers at the tip of a dripstone falls a mineral rain
Where pillars slowly rise and colored cones grow down
A dazzle in a cavern a colonnade of water clocks
Whose measurings have made sanctuaries in a rock
The metronomic sound the flowing spires keep and mark
   time
After blind descent a jeweled dimension to my buried
   selves
Curled and closed arms hugging knees

Attend
That moment when things move beyond themselves
  becoming more
The way a poem can raise worlds from the quiet page
Lift kites and cranes
In this deep way the lace-fans of great ferns and centuries
Of leaves sheltered in the press of time imprinted in a stone
Their foliate perfection moving upward
Growing from a rock to be the legend of lost trees

Always the hunter whose quarry is himself is driven down
A climber in caves a listener of long room under the hill
I hear my heart as stone's tumbling
A terrestrial monster caught in the rock-spill
I carved a ragged tunnel entered on all fours the final vault
To find on soaring walls the sacred painted animals that
  guard
The inner night
Brave in company of beasts I climb into the light

BETWEEN OUR LONGINGS AND THE MOON

Philippe Alexandre

The light rises on a small room; in a corner there is an old single bed (up stage left) with Francis on it, covered with a white blanket, tossing, turning and sighing. Between the bed and the small sink (up stage right), there is a crucifix on the wall. A chair (downstage right). Francis tosses and turns on the bed. He gets up, stops and stares at the crucifix for 1 second; then goes to the sink where he drinks a cup of water and comes back to lie down on the bed. A big sigh. He sits up looking at the crucifix.

FRANCIS:

The giver of sorrow and burns to my nights of drinks from cups of insomnia to my eyes: (still sitting on the bed, he turns to the audience) I found him on my way one raining morning, and I gave him out of my love a tap of pity and a little corner throbbing in my heart. Ever since, he has not left me once, or absented himself from my way. He followed me all over the great wide world; I wish I had not given him a single drop to drink on that morning. How can we forget pain, how can we forget him? We shall drink him, eat him, follow his erratic footsteps. As we sleep, his grim body is the last thing we see; his facial traits are the first thing we set sight upon in the morning; we shall carry him with us wherever our wishes and wounds carry us. We shall permit him to build dams between our longings and the moon; between our burning agony and the cool brook between our eyes and our sight. We shall permit him to spread sadness and sorrow in our eyes; we shall shelter him in an ecstatic nook of our songs' ribs, and finally the torrents of the valleys will carry him away and give him cactus thorns for a pillow. (softer) Oblivion will descend on the land; good evening sorrow, we shall forget pain..(5 seconds of silence. He is agitated.) But from where does pain come to us, from where does he come? He has been the brother of my visions from time immemorial, and the guide of my rhythms.

15

Yesterday, I took him to the deep waters and smashed him there, scattered him on the ocean's waves. I did not leave a sigh of him or a tear, and I thought I returned free from his arm: he would no longer cast sorrow on our smiles or hide bitter sobs behind songs. Then I received a red rose of warm fragrance from my beloved ones overseas. What did I expect to find in it? Joy and satisfaction. But it trembled and ran in warm thirsty tears, watering the sad tunes of my fingers. (<u>FRANCIS gets up, walks to and faces the audience while raising his voice</u>.) Can we not defeat Pain I ask you, postpone him till next morning or evening? Occupy him? Divert him with a toy or a song, or an old story of a forgotten tune? Who could that Pain be? A little tender child with questioning eyes, silenced by a lullaby and a loving pat? He sleeps as if I smile and sing to him. Who else but him closes his heart in the face of my sorrow and comes to me crying, asking that I love him? Who else but him distributes wounds, and smiles? (<u>FRANCIS goes near the chair but refuses to sit down</u>.) (<u>softer</u>) This little one...He is the most innocent of oppressors. Is he our loving enemy or our bitter friend? A dagger blow that wants us to give it our cheeks without reproach, without pain? Little child, pardon our hand and our mouth. You dig canals for tears in our eyes; we have forgiven your guilt and your harm from time immemorial; we have hidden you in our dreams, in every tone of our song. (<u>FRANCIS returns to his corner, sits against the wall his forehead resting on his arms. A din of a bell is heard from backstage. Dark</u>.)

CEREMONY

Gino Antonio

Calling for assistance
  for strength unheard of
  for spirits unseen
Evil has awakened
  evil has risen
  evil is near
Remember the stories
  recalling ancient songs, &
  rites of rituals gone past
Evil has come
  to take my soul away
  to take my inner wisdom
Memories of grandfather ways
  ancient ways still strong
  forget, and evil may last
Over and over again
  evil spells creating tension
  puts me under
Nurture the songs that play,
  the nature of the soul
  protection of young and old
Yearning for the morning after
  yen to be heard
  just like
  the smell of fresh morning dew
  following
  the cold, stormy rains
  the dark, spellbinding clouds
Through it all,
  strength regained
  songs and prayers remembered

Look, as
the lightning brings new light
to darkened skies
and hungry eyes
and listen, A strong roar rages
across open ground,
fills waiting ears
The Roar of Recharged Thunder

THE ELDER AND THE BAD APPLE

Gino Antonio

The wrinkles trace the years
  and, the other
  starts to embrace your fears

One old man, One bad apple
  and
  One park bench
  in
  this city of thousands
  All alone
  Silence is broken
  by
  not one word, but
  by
  One stare
  Silence has returned
  with
  many loud thoughts

    Just Listen

  With, sad tired eyes
  he says
  these wrinkles trace the years
  through heartache and
  all the tears

  through abandonment
  through unwanted silence
  disappointment after disappointment
  left behind and out-distanced

So alone with nothing
everybody is gone
Undying
still here for something

    Silently

with hurt angry eyes
he shows,
these scars embrace my tears
through heartbreak and
delinquent years

Thro gh punishment
through unneeded shunning
Resentment after resentment
left out and outlawed

So alone with nothing
Nobody is around
Unforgiving,
I'm still pushing towards something

They exchange an understanding
Wisdom given
Respect taken

With a defiant look
silently, he says
Oh, wise one sage
  Teach me your ways

With an uncompromising stare
silently, he expresses
Oh, Wild one with rage
  First, we spoil the whole barrel

The hand is really nothing
when the other, the fingers,
are somehow gone and missing
The bad apple is really something
when the other, the elder,
somehow shows what's missing

ROOTS

Gino Antonio

You are a seed
   deeply rooted in beliefs
   created by I, without fear
You
   recreate me when you
   look, me in the eye

You are a spirit of early dawn
   deeply nourishing our roots
   created by thoughts, from beauty
You
   restore my being
   with your warm thoughts

We are our
   own, earth and sky
   made to keep in harmony
   through the changing seasons
We
   reconcile, to seek shelter
   in, our flesh and blood
   to find,
   strength, love, and patience

Spirit of early dawn
   nurturing the sapling
   cherishing my thoughts
   with, warm rays
We
   grow stronger
   with blind faith and your beauty

I am a grown sapling
  with strong roots
  created from fearlessness
I
  work to recreate
  reinforced renaissance

Shil heh jeeh, Nhih Inaa
  Hoozhooh nishle
  Bi dzilii goh nishle
  Nizhoni goh nishle
  Hozhooh naahasglii
  Hozhooh naahasglii

YESTERDAZE

Gino Antonio

This is a little ditty about me, maybe you, or you know who having fun with someone, or somebody crying with no one doing who knows what, or whatever's doing what to who somewhere in my heinous nightmares, or in our everyday heavenesque fantasy called reality, that did it for the helluva it or doing it for every reason in the So-called book, and vice-versa, or Shit, that this was just a waste of words, paper, or time,   But who knows...

YESTERDAZE

Loco Hobo
Daily Ritual
Local Bozo
Nightly Ritual

Steal a lemon
Handful o' McDonald's salt
Bootlegged bottle, and
A Police chaser

Rancid garbaged dump
Last night's sacrifice
Premature offering, and
Innocent adolescent

Pretentious princes
The wannabe's and, Abusive
Promiscuous princesses
Make believe and, Illusive

2 x 4s and bats
Look of grimacing pain
Crowbars and collected hats
Exposed life, Crying shame

Looking for my monkey
Losing the ball n' chain
Found animal lunacy
Abusing shit for brain

Black n' White TV
"Calgon, Take me away"
Shattered TV screen
Jose, Show me the way

Lose the cap, Bro
Slice the yellow one
Palmful o' salt, Bro
Nice mellow shotgun
READY, SET, ESCAPE

Salt over the shoulder
Snort your sour away
Chase, shake n shiver
Worms' time to play
(DEEP BREATH)
Hellacious Utopia
Who Cares
About
Tomorrow Anyway

LUCID

Gino Antonio

In the ghostly night
  twisting and churning
  the ghost machine
  keeps turning

Friendly faces
  greeting your pain
  with
  the needles you're holding
  the gun they're pointing
  creating an illusion
  only visible to others
  trigger happy
  adrenalin junkies

Tossing and turning
  gears keep on
  rolling

Room for two
  in this
  One legged

  straight jacket chair
  Yourselves
  Tied down
  in
  your brain happy nightmare
  Skin crawling
  legs kicking
  Those
  demonic arms
  clutching leg irons
  and those

undying
death grip straps

Sweating and shaking
Phantom machine
overdrive cranking

Claustrophobia
setting in
your holding
on, for dear life
drowning
in, cold sweat
struggling
for, first light of day
screaming
in, silent lucidity

Gotta' wake up
this vampire night
Have to wake up
fangs and needles in sight

Wide awake
out of breath
One last shake
relieved to death

Gimme' back
My, Eagle bone Breast Plate
and
Leave
My, Virgin Nipple
Alone

SELF PORTRAIT BEFORE CANDLE LIGHT

Chris Apache   [To Galway Kinnell]

A window opens. Closes.
A draft of cold air brushes my back
while trying to awaken.

Out of the corner of my eye, movement
in trees behind a transparent
film finds a threshold on my limbs.

A kind of motion spinning endlessly, helix
twirling up my spine.
Am I scared?

My blood runs thick. Even now, before I
thought of my father.
Am I awake?

Can I not be careful to stop the will of it?

My answer came to me after being sick.
It said,
    "To bend to such strenuous living
     or breaking a simple
     principle is meeting an aortic complexion at
     point blank."

The louse still hangs in my mouth sack-like, as if to
prevent my last seeping breath.

What will I do?

I know there is emptiness inside. Though there may
be flesh, blood, bone and meat. It is still poison to me.

Dusk comes quickly and I see us
standing in a room of glass
up among the clouds
waiting for that same sickness to tell
us of last night when I was lost.

We greet each other with the vibrating faces
of war.

Which one shall I be this time?

There will always be the second. Standing
there always being second and the two
will never sever.

He may flutter across my mind to affirm my
existence or to change as a chrysalis would
and say he is there.

I may have ignored the sound of the cricket's
wings and played along with the idea that
he is simply an object of my perception.

The sound I hear now is a murmuring heart
beating a throbbing sound that may burst the
capillaries in my head. I turn away. I find
that if he is to hold up an object, then at some
point that object must slip and fall.
Which will create a sound that is deafening.

He spins spaciously. The sound is silent as sure
as I am red, it will kill me.
Am I lost?

He flings himself from me. Not far enough to be
distant,
close enough to cut.
Do I hear a beating rhythm or an old bone cracking
in its age?

That red face stares down on me to create this
illusion of an arm. His arm.
What will he do?

You race into my dreams and chase me into the weave
of your hair locks. Locking blank doors with
pad locks.
Closing. Open.

"...referring to drug dealers, users & ho-mo-sexuals
            including victims of AIDS
                            Anselm Hollo"

He dreams of boys' blue in pink beds racing for
the dawn toward tomorrows shady colors of
black and white.

What will I do?

Kali Ma comes bonding with paper and pen,
foaming from the mouth and God sits to
watch me drift away on a watering grave
and calls it a piece of ice.

My body contorts, bringing forth the colors
of an artist's brush. A mere stroke
chokes to call it me.

A purple ladder sways in the wickering light
spreading a conflagration of dark images
flying about the flame source and
he is still that child unwilling to play.

His eyes blink.
It is gone into a diminishing darkness of a
perfect perception.

My eyes open to find his footsteps in mine.
After his I see nothing, only another person
thought to be him.

He brings his tools for socializing and somehow
staples my mouth shut.
What can I say?

"...referring to drug dealers, users & ho-mo-sexuals
        including victims of AIDS
                                    Anselm Hollo"

A painful separation sets my house of old things aside,
somewhere in that forest
he still calls, "new growth."

I was hoping instead to leave him behind.

HE IS DEAD

Chris Apache

He was born with an eye
He wants to live a life
Not being touched
But touching others
With teeth-like finger nails that devour

He eats with those nails
At a table which leads
Him to believe
In a cannibalistic meal of violence

He pisses and spits his life down a can he calls, good

It is raining outside

He doesnt know that the rain that dampened my hair
Will threaten him like the drowning grass

Outside

Will he live
Or will he care

His life is a tunnel view, which leads him like a child
By the hands
In any direction of down
And his life is no honey pie

He remains to hide
Inside a premonition of a looking glass
And so vainly he tells me
He has not yet arrived
When will he come
When will he leave a world as bad as this (His)

He hears the tombstone
call out his name--and he wants to leave
As easily as it takes
A voice
To stress these sounds;

DRI NK   DR OWN

CO ME   HO ME NOW -- GRA VE A MENS

$$D \ R \ / \ I \ P$$
drip
down

DAD IS dead

He chooses not to move at all
Because he wants to be dead
Therefore he is declared dead
Limp head
Limp face
Limp hands
Limp feet

My stigmatic impulse to him is life
And if not there is no Christ
His salvation was buried with a man he calls, "Father"
He carries his style
And he too will fallow
Because their blood bonds to say
"Crime is a lonely child in the hallway"

                                    A
                    shaman's
                          casual
          ritual is
now in
                                          effect
New   dimension
                          opens
                            a
                          door

And I still write eulogies
For him

Dad is dead
     and
May he rest willingly

ALLEVIATE THE HEAD WORM

Chris Apache

A bitten hand in spite of dark skin
A driven force of giving waters
A foot full of energy
A head full of shit
I want to say eat your worm-filled shit so that it rots your
    head
So that you disappear from high rise buildings and fast cars
Disappear from your non-existent mouth and fight for your
    intellect
Savor the last taste of the meat's edge in exchange for a blade
    that carves my flesh into the shape of a flipping cat next
    door
You knew that day was coming when falling dirt would be
    your only stimulating motive
To spill your blood will hurt and dry out your bones
You continue to bury the children you never had
Your bones made of tough white earth weaken
You now walk with a limp
You kick your joints in place to creak again--crank your
    machine now because you won't be coming back.
Quick sow the seed which grows the worm so they won't
    wither and die
You assimilate into position and filter out the frightened
    ones, taking away
The gathering
The innocent
The heir
The son
You say go and it is gone
You walk and that energy explodes with my relatives inside
    you
One look and you humiliate me with the point of a finger
Then maggots poison the heaven made for you
You sift through my goods and stuff them in your pockets

You feed your hair roots with my saliva and leave me
    abandoned in a dream
You are that famine bringing Junta
You clean house and empty me into the streets
You clean house and throw me the scraps
You clean house and leave me clothes called hand-me-downs
You then kill me under the roof of the streets and dump me
    in your back yard to rot in the earth
You bite your hand in spite of your nothingness
You trample me through your tainted waters
You say you're full of energy, I know you're full of shit
I want to smash the head that holds the worm which says, "a
    chair is not a table"

BAN THE PSEUDODEMOCRACY

Milton Apache

Books are burning, the words are impossible to see through
    fire.
Impossible to hear, because your mouth is full of lies.
You blend the truth with dishonesty.
To form a hypnotic concoction of politics.
But i see through you, and your transparency shows.
The light has always been there, but you hid it with the
    curtains.
Now we will hide you.
Crawl back in the dungeons where you belong.
Taste the shit you have made for so long.
Eat it and let it reveal to you what you really are.
Die and settle on the cross that was built for you.

FERMENT ILLUSION

Milton Apache

Sadistic thoughts embedded
in a fictitious world of dead dreams.
To bring forth the demons of hell
and their righteous views
Would be reaping the embryonic mind of this fetus

Onslaughts of bubbled blood baths.
waver dreams of psychedelic acid and microdot
linger and sing songs to lonely housewives
who were mangled by the street and in their homes.

The dream keeper enters my dreams
and i forfeit the chance to froth at the mouth.
and say, "i'm not insane."
wrapped with cellophane wrappers
and flowers to cover the ignorance

Buried by the Hail Mary's
Turbine crushes you to a pulp
your body smeared over my canvas
as i paint you my world
with dancing witches, malicious remains
of the manhandled mannequin. Was it me?
inside the asylum?   My head?

"March yourselves," you say, "into The illusion room."
Where the Mother of Maids twists truth and reality
To make a fruitful drink of dribbled catgut

And my dog is me
Standing at the doorway
with broken bones and a shattered cranium
Brain enables to enact because it migrated
from my head to the floor
Bat hits home my cranium
bleeds internally

Nowhere to run inside my head
My eyes roll, then assemble
deep end flies off the handle

Wrapped in a ...
Wrapped in a ...

      Wrapped in a ...

Say farewell to my sanity
GOOD-BYE

FEAR THE WALLS FOR ONESELF

Milton Apache

I was writing you the day you went away
You left my head   twisted it wrung it   and hung it out to dry
I had the urge to scream
the bountiful pleasure of the high pitched octave
ringing outside my house. Like the bells at the St. Joseph's mission.
        screamed at you once
Nothing but the stir of the silence
I wanted to run to my home   the old cocoon
which shapes my life   into the form of an innocent rabid puppy
Standing outside my window, howling every two hours
CLOCK-WORK!   watchmen on the tower.
bellows its 2a.m.   4a.m.   6a.m. I couldn't sleep
waiting for you to return your self to my possession
        screamed once more
echos in the distance   bounce off walls, scratched records repetitive
tidal waves crash down upon, my head.
making me feel and taste nothing, but gurgled saltwater
Hide me in the corner, or the tiny cracks of eternity
so that i may not find myself.
And if i do, i might pump life back into myself.
THUMPTHUMP!   THUMPTHUMP!   THUMPTHUMP!
Shrink! Shrank! Shrunk!   my head   pinhead effect.
simply weaving my thoughts into an infinite space
where fear is reality
and reality made me blind
Allowing Karma to enter, first knocking on the front door,
then smashing through the back door
slapping my face, the sound of thunder as head slams pavement
For hell's sake I should yell for father, but I don't
Because my father died centuries ago, with the last falling star
I wished upon
When you stood outside my thoughts
waiting for me to bash your head
and call it art.

GLASS AND BONES

Milton Apache

SWACK LASH!
SWACK LASH!
Glass,   bones
tied to whips
stings the blood
That drips from
the mutilated back
flow to my feet
and stain them
I could remember it somewhere, Gazing out the window
on a cold and cloudy night. The sky for some reason was
drippy like a rose from a vine. The thorns from such beauty
crushes his skull sending
fragments
on the floor
lay porcelain
shards which
gives way to my
hands
nailed to the
crucifix
head slumped over
the sink. I noticed blood dripping from my hands
dead nerves dead hands underneath the shrouds of cloth
stuck to the decaying body
reveals nothing but, a dead man's cold look of stone
only to arise in three days and proclaim that he is king and lord

MECHANICAL MAN

Milton Apache

mechanical man
and the dead eye can see
yesterday   fall
with an explosion
  primrose pug   stood to bury me
with what she calls "good intentions"
The man with the patchouli oil
 and coffee stains
of the Aztec coffee shop
hands me a flower. "Don't worry   its all right."
words blasting from the soothsayer's mouth.
BUT IT'S NOT!
I feel your presence   breathing down
the small of my back
HOT!   COLD!   chilled goosebumps
twitched nerves   deadends frails
convulsive epilepsy
drags my brain across the floor
and drops my body to follow.
The next day I avoid you   I tried   but you appear
    you   your teeth   and wide smile
satin dress   innocent girl   wants to be
like
the old tree standing beside death
and doing nothing wrong
grotesque eye   looks at me lovingly
"Come to me you poor child!"
you hold me in your arms   you claw
and strip me of my old skin
but I shed a new one -- just for you.

DOWN THE COUNT

Milton Apache

10...
Such peaceful dreams   trail with blood
protein buildup   fills the incinerator room
the unbearable stench of the undead
Screams for hopeless life
melting lips grasp   grasping my throat
AAGCK!   AAGCK!

9...
Sensation
Burns my throat
reminding me of life in hell
my Hell was abandoned skyscrapers
crashing my head in my padded cell
I   wa   was
slapped against the w wall with only one life left
live it wwell   hope karma favors you

8...
Y y you   gouge at my eyes
threading yyourself   through my eye socket.
Preventing my sight   from actually seeing you.
W W weave your translucent self wwrap me into wh who
   you are.
But w who are you?

7...
I knew w wh h who I was
The penetrating head of the hammer
that passed me into unconsciousness
did not help much   either.

6...
you tried to manipulate me
with the feeling of vengeance
your pathetic rope burns
around my neck

5...
Deadly words entrance my mind
your game of fear tells me
i need a straight jacket.

4...
insanity transpares my body
m ma making me vulnerable
to the edges of razors
slipping into my flesh

3...
Numbness falls short
of reality

2...
in i i incision antonym for
                 de   ss cision?!
P   P P kids made me do i i it
L L oss Loss of...

1   11   11 11111 ....
scarred flesh tense
pa pA PARANOID
on the incinerator
it is time.

STAINED GLASS BECOMES MEMORY

Milton Apache

i came back to haunt you
Your mind deceived thoughts of passed times
when the crystal waters of the chandeliers   broke
To reveal what was left inside.
Nothing but the vast openness, and stench of rotting
    babies.
Only they wished, but never had a chance to live.
i felt the same, i wished
but you dug your own grave, made your own tombstone
i wanted the rose petals to fall at your feet.
i wanted you to lay in a silk or satin bed.
and you wanted the pine box instead.
The rainbow to arch over your head.
You wanted the opposite.   Always
the white clouds were given to you
Then you made thunder and darkened the clouds
installed the light fixture of lightning
it reminds me my head is cracking.
You were given the heavens you made it hell
And i gave it to you.

WEARING ITS INSIGNIA

Geraldine Barney

Wearing its insignia
with dignity
> The golden fluid
> seeks its way to
> delay me
>> and you.

1)   Impairment of indigenous minds.

2)   Contorted faces of children before birth.

And you want my thanks?

I'VE IMAGINED YOUR FACES IN THE ROCKS

Geraldine Barney

I've imagined your faces in the rocks
of the Chuska Mountains.

Petrified.

The rings of experience.

Something I cannot be.

WEDNESDAY, JANUARY 25TH, 1989

Neilwood R. Begay   (to grandmother)

The day started greeting the morning sunlight beaming through the open door. I would smell potatoes and fry bread as I looked through the smoke filled room at you. Uncle would make that funny surprised sound at my awakening. I washed and sat down for breakfast.

I can remember wearing a flimsy coat during the cold season. We heard the long cries of the birds living in the region. The plane flew high above and as I searched the sky you called to me from between cedar and pinon trees. The small flock of wounded sheep grazed in the field behind you, and you pointed into the heavens where the sound was coming from. I looked, I saw, and I looked back down to you with a smile on both our faces. You wore the tan corduroy coat and the usual skirt. Inside your black canvas shoes I knew you wore socks over your gum covered feet, because of the nasty blisters that bothered you when you walked. As I sat beneath a tree my thoughts were of you. As homesick as I felt I was happy to be with you on this day.

Back at the house a relative would make me cry. I would walk outside and weep in a pile of sand behind the hogan. You would come out and sit down beside me. You didn't touch my hand, you only looked far off into the distance, although your grey eyes could never see so far. You would apologize for them and tell me, "Awee ya anaalyeed. Your uncle and I need you to stay with us because we are too old to do the many things that you can do." Then you would sympathize with me by telling me that they shouldn't have been so rude for I was a good child, a good child who always helps out and a child who has parents that care. "I will take care of you until your parents come back for you. You stay here for now and help us out. Your parents will be back soon."

When all crying was done and relatives returned from where they came, you and I would start chores. Chores that werent needed to be done, like putting a pile of old boards up against the house. We didn't play, but with you, it was just as fun. I worked while you left to make dinner. Later I would be called in to eat. You sat on the floor, that was where the table was, as Uncle Tsosi and I sat on chairs. After eating uncle would always bring out a hidden can of soda. The three of us smiled and shared.

Evening came over us fast and beautiful. The Western sky lit up gold, yellow, orange, red, into purple and then night. As it did so, we sat outside, Uncle smoked and you spun wool. I would watch the both of your shadows moving until I could see no more.

MISERY LOVES COMPANY

Neilwood R. Begay

Another ceremony has been performed
I make my offerings
with nicotine cigarette smoke
as they rise and swirl
around you
I know the language of ceremonies
She brings humor into my room

She can stare at me
but she can't see me

Horses and rabbit
They are not what they appear to be
a man can have a wife
a wife can hold a man
I am the raccoon
I hear the ceremonies
they come to me
I lie here in NAVAJO
My thoughts here in NAVAJO
(I have an identity)

She stares at me
I am the raccoon

I have ceremonies too
I see them
a rubex cube in mixed colors
She tells me
She licked and sucked your poison
used it back on you
You hold the snake tongue in your mouth

Hold it
Your poisonous ceremonies
they do not work here anymore
perform them elsewhere
You see
We have our own Ceremonies too

THOSE THINGS SHOULD NOT BE SAID

Neilwood R. Begay

I will tell you
I know the taste of alcohol
the smell of fathers breath
I know deep secrets
they sweat in the palms of my hands   and
mother taught me
the power of silence in a translated language
to describe a one line
lonely song

Those things should not be said

Intoxicated
my memories
disease infected   and
these riddles are indefinite
whiskey shots have rotted my thoughts
with stains
I say in an almost silent whisper

Those things should not be said

I will tell you
who became me
sometimes even today
a child who
will not acknowledge mirrors
too ashamed to see
I look only into my eyes and blind out
the scars brought on by
my brow
my nose
my hair and my chin
the inherited letters line the edges
of my lip

Those things should not be said

I was born of water beside the water
during the time of water
I grew by the sensation of touches
to make my ways around
green subconsciousness
over powered by flame colored rays
I never asked questions
only silenced

Those things should not be said

I will tell you
There are moments now
washes, ravines and canals
filled with red waters   and I
tip my toes into these
imagine the times
like evaporations
from showers that race down
cool glass
my memories of a young home
I will tell you
I remember strands of hair
blinding my four year old vision
under a filthy grey blanket
in the white house with a red roof

Those things should not be said

You told me
At least one of us is getting somewhere
but
I speak for you
for each of you
when the burn of whiskey
has left the walls to bleed   or
when the vapors
have fogged our minds   and
when shame has deceived us into saying
once again

Those things should not be said

A ZUNI TURQUOISE FALSELY NAMED

Neilwood R. Begay

Your sensual immoral commands
to the world
(so appeasing to me)
the bounce of tangled hair
as you walk from the
opposite side of the room
at enormous speed
that could send a herd of
buffalos into a trot and
Black magic
defeated with your lyrical words

In ignorance
to slam you into an inconvenient corner
might have
left you breathless
Yet you defeated my commands and
moved toward the center of the room

A Zuni turquoise falsely named

In naiveness
you fanned your smoke
to aroma
my jasmine tea
and only
hindered me

Zuni turquoise
you live in a room
filled with lush pillows
that *Neglects* to embrace
all commands

PERSISTENT
Neilwood R. Begay

Rhythms from a guitar
  heard from a second room
     on the next floor
Moving tangles of chords
  pulling and vibrating
     into fading strums

Circles enlarge
     in repetitive waves
  The sky is an aura of lavender
   over rust colored lights
   silhouettes of autumn
     trees and remains of
      summer leaves

White porcelain cat
     trimmed in gold and the
  Persistent clock
     Silver   the color of time is silver
      pasted on
      a smoke filled pane glass window

Lyrics   the Spanish man
   his voice fades
     under strumming chords

His first name is Earl   his last is Grey
  he looks at corn colored beads
    with black and copper stones
    as a black cat with blue eyes
        watches on
Her first name is Liza   her last is Minnelli
  she smokes cigarettes on my wall and...

...the sun rises earlier today
       it is still yesterday   seven after seven
                    to be correct...

...she looks at me through a crystal ball
       hanging on a wire cord

Why won't you call me anymore?

Their names are   Moorea
               Trista Pena
                Passion
          My favorite is   No Volvere
they are beautiful lyrics who
       never need to be painted in words
      so that I may understand
their father allows me to imagine and feel
           the beauty
       of each daughter

A blue light cuts through smoky purple
      show me if there is a heaven
        Why can't I be with you?
        Give me a strand of turquoise wrapped in
          silk affections of your love
     Don't lie anymore
       Touch me and mean it
         Kiss me and feel it
I'll pierce an ear and wear a lock
     of your hair
       so that I may hear you whisper
                    in my ear

I'll carry your nails
  so that I may kiss your fingers
    before bed each night
I'll rob your pillows of breath
  so that I may dream your dreams

Think of me tonight and wish for me
  Smell my fragrance tonight and miss me
      as I   miss you
            tonight

HAADEE'SH NANINA?

Neilwood R. Begay

I found you torn In two
   Ha'at'iish nizhi?
   They may have rended your name
      they couldn't subvert your soul
Your heritage called my silent forgotten name

  Shi yaazhi you told me
    Shika iinlyeed
 I have been cast aside
 I have nowhere to turn
    no place to call my own

There is more history in you
  than there is   I see in me
  Your colors   displaced and worn
      the colors I cover everyday
        I try to understand
  Your hair with streaks of gray
Haash yiindza?
  You silently stare
     Haisha' honiila?
  Your own grandchild has gotten away
     I will help you
To learn of who I am
To understand what they have unto you
     effects me in this way
  Shima yaazhi
    I will always come to you
    to hold faith of what little knowledge I have
Your features significantly line
  every deprived vessel of my Navajo Ways

I HAVE A VOICE

Molly Shackelford-Bigknife

I have a
VOICE
language all my own
it is not in
your tongue
it is in my own
If you try to
HEAR ME
in ways you are accustomed to
you will only hear
SILENCE
But if you
JUST LISTEN
abandon preconception
I will show you
who I am
LISTEN WITH YOUR SPIRIT
you will hear my voice
and though
I don't speak words
you will
UNDERSTAND

THE SOFT MID-NIGHT CURES OF A TURTLE CLAN, PRISONER

Annissa Dressler

Remember the clock of hypnotists
How I wanted to recreate that honestly
porcelain china box folded in your end table.

 Cried, wrapped in white cords, wanting an
electric explosion of you to kill me.
Drove through the parking lot in 90 degree lamp shades
to find you in the 7th letter of this white man's
alphabet   Iroquois
Twisted the last cigarette until it lasted of
cures and I felt better, I'm
 on the second to the last drag
today...

Her walls were meeting grounds.
I scratched messages with clay blades
for you to find when blind
folded

You still can't read braille
can you?

Dying for that low tied extreme
of passions day, knowing the box
       high passions sun wasn't full.
You were empty
by then
by here
 and there.

I grabbed your elbow   leather
fist and poured tide water down
your throat, it rises to a pink
 moons peak,

60   no stanza break

yet you couldn't read the texture of my skin to
know   I was saying, "stay."

The turtles sensation of braille numb
and curing cigarettes burning between our fingers, just one
last drag.

 One last drag, one last high, one last eye of that
watch of steam,
just one more drag, drag through those
caves, her caves, curing caves, white turtle houses.

You still can't read braille.

The buffalo room is mine,
We divide into halves and I
take both pieces of your dream, my
friend now.

    could never think
this open book of you would ever be
read better.

One more drag, reaching the filter, no more 6am calls.
It was just bad timing
  no more red halls for cures.
The moving van is outside
spurting your name
waiting to drive you from an Indian Katchina
to an Indian Katchina.

My hands are red and cupping
closed to the taste of your
texture, spiderman, I can
read braille.

This cigarette is curing.
It's just another emotional
claustrophobia, stuffing open
stitches.

Ashtrays of cures, drying in this sun full
time, just one more drag, they all want to burn again, in
    closed halls
and between our fingers.

Ashtrays of turtles, in a 11 month blue cup,
If I am regaining
sight you are just another
  mute recovery man.
turtle dreams in this
fish clan girl.

YOU ARE WINDOWED

Annissa Dressler   for Travis

We talk cups
and how cup surrounds
and lays on the chest for coloring,
cupped.

Seeing blue cups, masculine
A fuchsia cup over and between
the mouths of men. I didn't
expect you to bite.

Bite open cups of other
colors, hoping to find a
political muddy resolve.

How dare you.

How dare you sit in that
shelf of brown unopened cups and watch
  us melt to a shifty red,
bleeding at the hand of you unmolded
shitheads.

How dare you reglaze yourself.

ALONE WALKING

A. A. Hedge Coke

there
has always
been   no one
when
there most
definitely
should   have
been   someone
here   to ease
hardships
endured   thru
this walk
and someone
could   have
definitely
been   there
when
no one
always   was
there

JEFF KAHMAKOOSTAYO

ROSE SPAHAN

JEFF KAHMAKOOSTAYO

SHIRLEY MARES

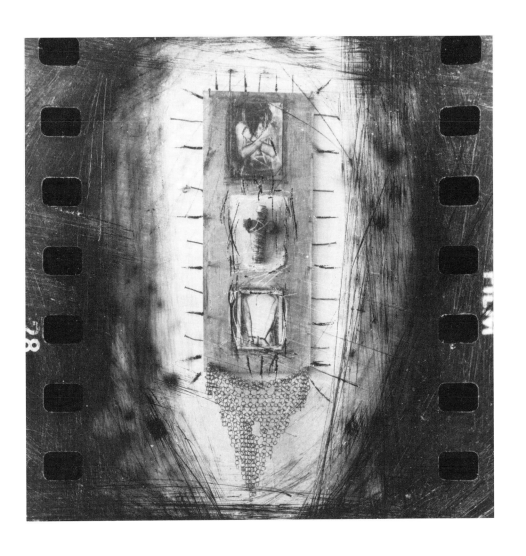

DA-KA-XEEN MEHNER

JAMES NEPTUNE

JAMES NEPTUNE

JEFF KAHMAKOOSTAYO

WOKIKSUYE

A. A. Hedge Coke   in memory

Like a horse's tail
so thick, black
down past his waist
beautiful. Wayanka.
Chemotherapy -
white man's
man made cancer ...
doesn't distinguish
between good or bad
cells ... just kills.
The spirit is connected
to the hair at the
crown - pahiŋ hočoka.
The hair falls
the spirit goes,
the will is
connected no more.
Leukemia -
cancer of the
White
Blood Cell.
Lakota wičaša
Oglala wiča
Ha Luta Oyate wičozani šni
Kuja, unšika
Caŋku Wakaŋ o mani
ma wanagi o mani

wašigla
čeya
wokiksuye
wokiksuye
wopilamiya
miksuya
Caŋku Luta o mani
Caŋku Wašte o mani
wohitika
iyomakpi, iyomakpi
ake - ampetu
ampetu wašte
I knew him well.

REFLECTING WIND AND RAIN

A. A. Hedge Coke

reflecting
unlikely wind spinning controversial force
kicking rain facing danger
enclosed in
travelling cloud
pouring
destiny and probability
unfolding
lives   challenging
touch of earth
settling in its time
on weary place
to journey
unrelentlessly continuing the
climb backward
to crimson sky
of morning
and of mourning
crosscutting
moist tears
droplets forming
on sadness
and smile
dancing harder
obtaining
knowledge
leaning just
a tiny inch
further toward
change occuring
in the most
mysterious and
compelling
difference in

no stanza break

calling wind
moistened in song
and against
emotions in your
eyes suddenly
again reflecting

THUNDER HAWK MELTDOWN

A. A. Hedge Coke

pulsating rhythm
like a hoofbeat
on traditional drum.
off-siding center
gravitational force,
flinging balance,
unsettling logistics
of perceivable
imagined reality.
without warning
all preparedness
slips off like
a wave of peeled
onion skins
falling to the floor
in ripples and
ripples up my spine
stimulating
cardiac and mental content
to the heartbeat
and dance I restrained,
yet survives,
when you cast
me aside like
I was token,
or teasing.
that which has the strength
to endure
flooding this shell
in burning torrent,
ripping protection
to shreds of humility.
begging pity
in   uncontrollable

urge   to find
relief from passion
in the folds
of your extremities.
driving beats
from the left chamber
of true   emotional desire,
from my chest
up my throat
making it impossible
to swallow
past the obstacle
you say doesn't exist -
yet pounds
moving the
blue   green
pendleton shirt,
swaddling the
tornado
you overlooked,
in your quest
for someone   to
care for only you
and hold you
above   reason.
just now   you
appeared   at my
door,   head down,
those incredible
brown eyes raised,
you uttered
"hou."

THE MANTIS

A. A. Hedge Coke

during my sleep
you approach
slicing space with
iron antennaes
and arms of steel blades
The Mantis
The Manipulator
Praying for Prey
devouring heads of
those less aggressive
and more progressive
I tense, adrenalin rushing
filling blood and arteries
with strength
coil and recoil
preparing jab and hook
just upon verge of defensive strike
I wake

NIGHT IN CHAOS

A. A. Hedge Coke   for Sandy & Clay

Tires squealing
like rubber screams
fire flashing
from the barrel
A few choice words of English
in a barrage of Spanish
Blinds rise and slide open
faces peer into the night
Babies cry from jolted sleep
and boys run across the streets
looking at broken glass and metal
Where ARE the mothers?
I hate you! I'm going to kill you!
No, I'm going to kill you!
Puta, BITCH, STUPID MOTHER-FUCKING BITCH!
No, Don't . . . DON'T, please, ple--
Screaming of a different kind
Stucco and window shatter interrupting
private affair with gang warfare
flashing from low-rider's cherry ride
escalating terror
she looks for her make-up

TOSSING THOUGHTS

A. A. Hedge Coke   for C.N.V. & J. Lam

Tossing thoughts on paper
over your shoulder
Releasing pain and frustration
throwing anguish and desire to the wind
Capturing precise image
in broken language
800 AD Chinese poet
20th Century Apache man
Shared drink and communicado
between spirit, dual entities
Patrons and peers in audience
honoring genius past
condemning genius present
Messages borne upon word
filter through vessels polluted by drink
and only one sees connection between both of you

SHOE GESTAPO AT THE BLUE LIGHT SPECIAL PLACE

A. A. Hedge Coke   for Ruth and Garth

Blue Light Special Place
Indian Heaven
innocently Stoney Woman picks up
a pair of shoes for her niece
checks in to check out counter
scanners beep and register difference in price
accusatory insults flash in clerk's light eyes
shoe gestapo summoned and arrives in authorative walk
customers growing concern, impatience and popping sweat
gestapo checks down pricing charts
friend to Stoney Woman demands explanation
Shoe Gestapo Man of the Blue Light Special Place
whispers, "How are You?"
Allright! Mr. Authority's a skin, too
checking chart with concealed smile
she's cleared
she's relieved
check out girl sneers anyway

TWO CROWS LAUGHING

A. A. Hedge Coke   for Psa, Jack, J.R., Travis, and Vaughan

Patient Man looked out upon a grey world. The light upon his face cast shadows between the center of his nose and his left ear. Patient Man had long black hair and long, striking, features. His eyes were dark and black like a raven. His left eye, the eye he talked with... the right eye, he listened with. Patient Man was a young full-blood in white man's clothes. Patient Man had wisdom within from his experiences in life. The people often came to Patient Man, even at such an early age, for counsel. He showed great leadership ability in many aspects and was remembered specifically for his storytelling skill.

Once Patient Man told me the story of Two Crows Laughing. I will tell you the story he told me now.

A half-blood girl child ventured into the woods on the hills over the Tickling Creek. She became lost while looking for choke cherries and sat down to rest near a cottonwood tree. Not being exactly over-concerned with losing her way she began to busy herself breaking twigs of cottonwood at the joints to reveal the stars inside the stems.

After some time she heard some voices that crackled like very old people talking. These voices were high above where she sat resting and breaking cottonwood. She listened to see if she recognized the voices. The half-blood girl could not understand the words of the language they spoke and became alarmed. She worried that it might be an enemy or a gi-gi coming. The voices grew louder and louder and she realized by their tone that they were talking about her. She tried and tried to locate the source of the voices but couldn't.

Half-blood girl became so frightened she cried out to them for pity as they were beginning to make her feel she was going mad hearing them and being unable to see them.

The voices grew into a laughter of mockery and sarcasm. She cried out to the animal world and spirits surrounding her and even to the trees and plants to help her.

Deep under the ground a council of ants heard her pleas and the ant people took up their evening flutes and began calling for the sun to set earlier in order to help her in her circumstance. The ants climbed up from their kiva and played to the sun, bidding it rest for a night and release the darkness-sun to the sky.

The clouds gathered in the west over the farthest red butte you can see from here, where I am telling you this. And the sun, who was very sleepy from the ant flutes, ducked down into the horizon so that the moon would be released to the night sky to keep the stars company.

High above, in the cottonwood tree, two crows (who had been mocking the little girl) lifted their wings and buried their heads beneath their folds to roost for the duration of the night.

Half-blood girl thanked the ants and the moon and sun and even the crows for teaching her to be cautious about straying away from her people and promised to make a give-away to show her thanks. She eventually found her way home by following the stars she recognized and told this story to Patient Man, who told it to me. I remember this story and Patient Man whenever I see a beautiful sunset fall on that red butte, the same way it is now. That is why I told you.

RAINING EYES

A. A. Hedge Coke   for Stephanie

I woke up with raining eyes and held myself still until I felt
control, then I slipped down from the bedframe to the floor
being very careful not to wake my brother and sister. Already
the smell of *a di ta s di* caressed the morning air, taking away
the dusty odor and replacing it with smooth mint.

The wind slammed the screen door, across the room from
where I stood against the wall. Where we had been staying
with my dad's brother since social services almost took us
from my dad. I didn't see my uncle as I crept down the hall;
his wife was in the kitchen making pan bread. She never did
notice me, so it was easy to get by her unseen.

Finally I'm outside, the coolness feels good on my skin and
I want to run. All kinds and colors of birds fly by singing. I
feel free. I can hear their wings beat. I run for a long time
and I stop at the store where some kids get pop and candy.

Inside the store, the floor is rough oak; a ceiling fan keeps
the air moving and clicks light into shadows that flicker all
over. No one seems to notice, nor do they notice the dust
stars in the sunlight me and my brother play with when its
really hot and we're very bored.

I slip around the counters filled with boxes of food. Many
of them are covered with dust because they're too expensive --
jacked-up prices. A man, a white man, cuts up meat with a
big cleaver. He's missing some of his fingers on one hand
and he's very fat from us having to live off of his store.

I'm really happy because no one has seen me all day and I
know I can reach out and grab the biggest, juiciest plum in
this rack and put it into my pocket, palm it in my hand and
leave the store very slowly, calmly, and go back down to the
curve on the road and sit down to eat. Wild plums grow right
here, but they're still bitter yet.

In the distance, at my uncle's house, I see much men
coming and my heart goes up to my throat and its beating
moves my shirt. All I can imagine is that my dad has come to
take me home.

I throw the pit into the ditch and run like the horses we ride--long strides, smooth, legs that feel like they're flying between steps, eyes straight ahead, hair blowing back...

I see a man. He looks like my dad, but he's different. This man is old and he's the only person that has looked directly at me all day. He's smiling, but I'm scared. I stop. I don't want to be close to him. I think he's a ghost or someone tricking me to make me think he's my dad. My dad isn't that old; it hasn't been that long. I only grew out of shoes once this time. I run back to the curve in the road and my eyes fill with rain again.

My uncle comes to me and tells me to go back to the house, that there are more uncles there now, more of my dad's brothers. I don't want to look at the one that's old, he scares me . . . too much like my dad. It's too scary.

Maybe I'm afraid my dad will be that old before social services lets us go back to him.

He always has to save me from her anyway, all of us, she'd kill me if I'd let her . . . she would. I know she wanted to when she beat me with that broken black metal telephone. I still have knots on the back of my neck from that night before they took her away and tried to put us in a foster home.

While she was beating me up her voice got louder and sicker and the *s* sound of her words got sharp on her false teeth. No matter what I do, I can never get away from that sound. I have tried every way I know how but, even when I cover my ears with my hands and hum, or sing with my head buried under the blankets -- it hurts my ears . Sometimes I even dream that voice and those *s* sounds. That night she screamed, "I hate you and I've hated you since the day you were born!" over and over again. Finally, she quit hitting me because she was more interested in listening to herself scream, or something, and I got loose and ran outside and waited in the ditch beside the road until my dad came. I told him. I told him everything. I hated to, but I couldn't take it anymore.

He took me for a long drive in his '63 Plymouth Fury . . . white with red seats . . . then we stopped where he said his relatives used to stay. Nothing was left to show that they had lived there, nothing stands now . He found a web on a tree and put it on my worst cut to stop the bleeding and we walked a while. He picked up some smooth black stones and gave them to me to hold; they were very cool and I felt like they were taking away all the things I had inside me that made me hurt. He offered me his hand, in friendship, like I was grown and I rested mine in his, gently, just for a second and then we went back to the house. He went inside and told her she was going to go away again and he called them to take her away, from the pay telephone down the road.

I sat on the ground and watched them take her away . . . kicking and screaming and blaming me for everything . I wanted to pity her, but I pitied him more. I miss my dad and I wish he would stay here with us. He would never want to put his brother out that much though and there are all of us here already.

I remember that day clearly. I look up at my uncle still waiting for me and he smiles, just a little bit. I get up and he takes me to his brothers at the house. He tells me again that they're my uncles that maybe I had seen them before. If I did I must have been too young to remember. I don't want to look at their faces, just in case they all look like my dad, so I look at their feet instead . . . then, I go help his wife with bread and coffee and mint tea and say nothing.

When I'm done, I look out at the hills and watch the wind hit the grasses, like waves in water and I imagine the grasses are running, like me . . . always running, but staying in one place . . . waiting and running.

STANDING BEFORE ME

A. A. Hedge Coke   to the Faculty and Students at IAIA

Standing before me
wrapped loosely in red blanket
tears streaming across
the bones of your cheeks
your head remains high

Waiting behind you
mounted proudly upon strong horses
 staffs rising across
the blue depths of sky
society of warrior call

LIKE A WHITE SHELL

A. A. Hedge Coke   for Ernie and Jim Elk

          Like a white shell washing upon shore
again she rises in changing tides
Extending wisdom to dancing nations
path of proud and pitiful
lečiya o wiokipi
lečiya o wiokipi
seventh generation awaiting celebration
renewel coming with calf woman
completing circle, intertribal reconciliation
creation, way of life
sacred hoop once broken
spirit, star nation,
sacred woman your blessing
               in purification now mends

BORDERLINE

A. A. Hedge Coke   for Grandma & all my Canadian friends & relatives

shared distancing
in circumstance
pulls   magnetizing
poles away   from
barriers
gravitating   toward
native freedom
currently under
red, white and blue
persecution
and crowned   maple leaf
oppression
erasing imaginary
boundary lines
separating
relation indigenous

POSTCARD IMAGES

A. A. Hedge Coke   for Amy, Donna, Alvin, Carmen, & Carmen

Beneath the fauna
eyes of truth, innocence
Behind the shoulder
eyes of greed and horror
persuasion of oppression
eyes that prey
hands like talons
stillness, concentration
preserve the culture
no reaction
no assimilation
Behind the shoulder
Disappears like smoke
Beneath the fauna

PLEAS

A. A. Hedge Coke   for Charmaine and all the children

Guided by
learned behavior...
rung on ladder,
score on page,
chapter in book...
destined children,
future generations...
the lucky ones...
unaffected by
FAS .... FAE
search as their
parents once searched
for the warriors
for the strong women
accomplished and respected
to mother and father them...
THE ORPHANS
of assimilation and
of the drink of
dissention, weakness
and misery.
If strength and wisdom
are to be reclaimed
and justice committed...
Who among us stands
to fill the empty role
of role - model?

QUESTIONS TO AN ANTHRO

A. A. Hedge Coke   for Wesley A. Black Elk

Why is it   when you study your own people,
white past,   you call yourself historian?
Why when you study ours,   red past,
do you call yourself anthropologist?

What would you think of an all
Indian anthropologist group going to
Europe to dig up your grandmas
to check out her clothes
or to L. A.'s Forest Lawn
to dig up hippies from the sixties
to find out what caused the LSD craze or Jesus Freaks?

Why do you think you have the right to speak for anyone
Who is capable of speaking for themselves
and would prefer to do so?

Are you intimidated by REALITY
and do you know when to Quit?

LET PRETENTIOUS FREEDOM RING

A. A. Hedge Coke   for M. Noe

Compartmentalizing   acknowledged correlations.
Linkage of fibers   weaving mainstream tapestry,
containing proud Americans historical accomplishments,
    let pretentious freedom ring.
1890 . . . leading national heros
organize   apple pie, hot dogs, and the Brooklyn Dodgers.
Compartmentalizing   unacknowledged correlations.
Trail of frayed promises tearing apart survival,
way of life, devastating proud Native Peoples
respectful accomplishments
    let pretentious freedom ring.
1890 . . .   leading national heros
organize theft, genocide, and such massacres as Wounded
    Knee.
Compartmentalizing mainstream Americans,
continue to claim . . . in complete undying faith . . .
no current correlation to crimes committed
by the   perpetrators of Manifest Destiny
guaranteed by the biblical prophets historical page
in belief that these Americans were a different people
The United States of America, based on religious freedom
and shopping malls
    let pretentious freedom ring
1776... Native Freedom of Religion Act delayed until 1979...
Medals and honors bestowed upon the 7th Calvary match in
correlation to those bestowed upon the Brooklyn Dodgers.
Apple pie, hot dogs, baseball, heros, and genocide.
Product and part of the assembly line accomplishments of
historical value in Mainstream American pride.
    Let pretentious freedom ring.
1991 . . . leading national heros
take Indian names, claim reincarnation from Native spiritual
    leaders,
mimic war cries during ball games . . .
Redskins, Braves, Warriors, Chiefs . . .

86

parody sacred ceremony in automotive industry
Sundance, Thunderbird, Cherokee Chief, Dakota, Cheyenne..
Is compartmentalization   technique   in assimilation,
in destruction,   in persecution?
We the People, United we stand . . . words taken directly from
    Native constitution
from sea to polluted sea.
    Let pretentious freedom ring.

DIGS

A. A. Hedge Coke   for my dad & Dehl

The rusted clasp of the faux-gold poison ring broke just
when Stephanie peeled back its cover to investigate its
contents. It was, as were all the others, completely empty and
she laid it next to dozens of duplicates on the grey metal shelv-
ing case in the work lab in the Anthropology Department at
Northridge University. Professor C. Thompson, an older native man from the northeast coastal region, peeked around
the corner observing Stephanie. The professor watched these
tiring field testings which, at this time, were without result
as far as the faculty was concerned, but promising enough in
theory to continue with complete funding from the B.I.A.

He took special note of her physical appearance to deter-
mine her fitness for such stressful activities. Stephanie was a
small woman, medium build (from the east coast too, though
more southern), with black hair cut into a punk cut reminis-
cent of traditional men's styles from the 1800's. She layered
the black with dyed-in crazy colors of red and hot pink. The
shocking effect gave her round face an angular look and accen-
ted her dark almond eyes. He saw that instead of becoming
fatigued she seemed to find satisfaction and joy in the tasks.

The project underway was initiated by a large concerned
Indian movement group from the California coast. The site of
the dig was Forest Lawn Cemetary in Los Angeles. Almost six
months into the dig approximately 70 burial spots had been
unearthed. Most of these graves were close relatives of the
rich and famous who had passed on poor and destitute in the
60's. The exact intent of the project was to find conclusions
as to the cause and effect of the rise of hippies and psycha-
delic drug usage in that particular era...also, possibly, to
locate evidence of reasons for certain fashions and fads such
as the mini-skirt and cultural behavior and practices, as in
electric rock. Focusing on documented and well-known drug
users and freaks was deemed the most practical approach to
discover factors pertaining to this under-culture outbreak of
the Euro-American Invader/Intruder Tribe. The People
(who under assimilation utilized the trades, skills and con-

88

cepts of the Invaders) now saw clearly their true benefit and the benefit of applied western sciences, in general. Almost one-hundred people found gainful employment on this specific dig alone. That gave promise to hope in these dim times of fallen real estate value and sympathetic Mainstreamers organizing benefits to feed people in another continent (any proceeds left after overhead costs, of course).

Stephanie's thoughts were concentrated on extracting evidence to base new theories on. She had received numerous phone calls and letters claiming to have leads to insight in these happenings of the 60's from people "who were there". But, she knew tribal people--especially ones who witnessed an era--were never to be taken seriously, or trusted for information. The Invader tribe--although responsible for bringing these philosophies and concepts to the People--especially couldn't be trusted. To remind the freshmen students of this the dean of the Euro-American Anthropology Department ordered all rolls of toilet paper in the lab and work areas to be printed with stark white lettering on sky blue background to read U. S. TREATY PAPER with stars and stripes on the borders.

Secretly, she hoped that in being close to their bones and belongings and discovering data to log into their official history she might herself grow to be like them. She idolized the 60's especially...beatniks, LSD, disposable dresses and cigarette lighters, princess telephones and performances in which you could completely destroy instruments and be considered a musical genius, peace and love to cover up war and genocide...she became mesmerized in the dream that she could be greedy, possessive and an aggressor to be proclaimed a heroine and immortalized. She even pondered the possibility of happening upon a ghost of a Euro-American, in which, she could emulate and claim the name of,to trick her peers out of the wages they earned. Maybe they would build a statue of her in a park or blast a mountain into pebbles save the replica of her image for all time.

These images brought many smiles to her face as she deliberately showed utmost care and responsibility in the examination of goods looted from the corpses of the Invaders and Intruder's descendents the Mainstreamers which were lined-up on wire hooks and strung suspended across the ceiling of the entire 2nd floor in the Anthropology building. The building temperature kept at a flat 50 degrees helped keep her alert. Climate control being another great gift of the Intruders for the People to enjoy comfort from all weather... good or bad.

It hadn't always been this easy. She remembered her mother horrified to discover her own grandmother's remains catalogued in the museum at the University of Tennessee and all the other people of the older age......(those before the premiere of *DANCES WITH WOLVES* and the 21st century REAL assimilation, those of the People who she now recognized as Hold-Outs) tears and despair of oppression. She remembered crying with her mother and protesting in written article the anthropologists specializing in American Indian studies. But, that was before she became enlightened.

Stephanie was deeply embarrassed by her previous choices in behavior and her inherent naivete. Now that she was enlightened with Euro-American philosophy she understood their crude attempts at finding evidence for theory by digging up corpses... one must be close to the bones and remains of the dead to understand another race, even a very primitive race such as the Euro-American and its clanships and bands.

Even the bands and clanships made sense to her now. Based on wealth, instead of blood, the blue-collar, white-collar and newer grey-collar workers spoke in similar languages but with very distinct dialects pertaining to their field of labor.

Stephanie had set a career-goal for a five-year plan toward being the first Native woman anthropologist studying Euro-American culture to travel to Europe and initiate a mass dig of remote cemeteries internationally. The project she dubbed

90

EARLY MIGRATION STUDIES and it asked the question why Europeans travelled across the ocean to The Peoples' Land instead of improving where they originally were, or walking across the Bering Straight as they seemed to be of general belief that the People had during a thirty year period in which the land may have been joined by shallow ridges or sand bars. She also planned another dig and study of members of the royal families to study why Europeans travelled to the Middle East to find religion and then tried to force their beliefs on all other peoples of the earth (a practice still continuing today on network and cable television).

Stephanie remembered her childhood teachings and oral history from her grandfather. She recalled being horrified , also, at the thought of Andrew Jackson's Tennessean men basting meat in the grease they rendered from Creeks' corpses which they had burned to death--unarmed--in their own cabin... not too long before his election to Presidency and of Colonial Euro-Invaders ordering heads of Chiefs served to them on silver platters. Now that she received educational enlightenment she understood that in order to subdue nations one must be blood thirsty in quest, yet publicize through literature and written historical accounts that it was the other way around. And she understood why Jackson is on every twenty dollar bill in circulation even now.

Yes, Stephanie was assimilated and formally educated and gifted in her works and talents. Professor Thompson was delighted in hand-choosing her for this tedious work. It was more to both of them than just another labor. He watched with great pleasure as she finally found a minute trace of LSD behind a picture of the Beach Boys in a locket from the corpse of a nineteen year old California girl.

As the discovery made was announced on the 10 o'clock news, a full bottle of St. Pauli Girl beer smashed into the newscaster enclosed in screen suspended from the ceiling beams over the bar in a local Yuppie Mainstream English Pub on Reseda Blvd.

91

CRUCIFIED JESUS

A. A. Hedge Coke

for Derya

C'mon into my garage. Why? Well... God told me to do it one day while I was driving my truck. He impressed the thought in my mind. I immediately stopped off at a store and bought some toothpicks, glue and tweezers and went to work in my garage. God told me to make a toothpick statue of a crucified Jesus and Amanda Donohoe has me living in fear.

I will have to start from the beginning. You may have read about me in the National Enquirer, "Bob Haifley (it's the picture with a mostly bald white man with light eyes and a grey-streaked beard--that's me) is creating a toothpick effigy of Jesus in Toothpicks! etc..." Here, let me put this last toothpick on... Over five years ago, I began sculpting a figure of our beloved Lord Jesus Christ from his father's craft in Minature. Yes, his daddy was a carpenter and I use only real 100% wooden toothpicks in my Jesus. I have spent over 2,500 hours all together constructing him in life-size (or bigger, nobody knows exactly how big he really was) style.

At one time I was losing my ability to reason and I sat down and prayed, Lord, you're gonna have to show me how to do the hair. I got up and right away I bent some of the toothpicks to apply and it worked just right. There are over 10,000 toothpicks on the hair alone, all in all, there are about 65,000 toothpicks of various sizes... but, all white, of course.

Now, I never went to no art school and I sure ain't got no picture of the real Jesus, but he is in the statue. You can see him for yourself. I keep him hung up, same way he was back then, feet nailed together... crown of thorns and all against a black background with a spotlight for special effect.

My neighbor, Henry Ramos, swears his breath leaves his body when he looks at my toothpick crucified Christ. The honorable Rev. Charles Wickman of Christ Community Church in Monrovia, California called my statue a marvelous miracle piece of artwork. He says it's like a sense of something spiritual. I know God wanted me to build his only son. It's my tribute to God. All I want in the world is to display the Jesus in a church, or at a state fair, somewhere. Now, that's what I want. But, then there's that Amanda Donohoe, who I mentioned earlier, the bisexual attorney on LA Law... you know, the one that kissed that Michelle Greene right on prime time television... Now, she's threatening the existence of my Jesus. I am terrified others will follow her madman antics in a crazed frenzy and spit on Jesus' everywhere. Just like she spit on that crucifix in the movie *LAIR OF THE WHITE WORM*. She claims she enjoyed spitting on Jesus... it was a thrill to her. I have decided to paint my Jesus with fiberglass resin to protect the wood fibers from moisture, it also makes white wood turn a beautiful golden color...for more added beauty. Claiming she's delivering a message against the church, Christ and Christianity committing atrocities against women throughout history. She says she will continue using her roles for such statements.

Now, what exactly do you suppose will happen when our youngsters see such nonsense? You know how easily misled they are. They will most likely go and use it for an excuse to go wild and use her ideas to vandalize Jesus figures nationwide. And who can stop them? GOD WILL. He told me so. He said it could take some time though, being he's so busy and all... I'm just living in fear that she'll get to my Jesus before God has a chance to come back to my garage, or to my truck.

There are those in the world that are good and those that are sinners. The bad people in the world defy God... she's one of them... Me, I don't feel sorry for no one that has a mind like that... no, sirreeee... and I will protect my crucified toothpick Jesus with my life... I will even resort to violence in an army of God-fearing men, if I must, to protect my crucified Jesus of toothpicks. God did want me to build this... he did. Amanda, wherever you are you had better learn to fear what you spit on and to stay in Los Angeles where you belong... don't you come near Monrovia or, my Jesus, I'm warning you!

Oh, by the way... could you spare a toothpick... I've got this little bit of apple peel stuck in my uppers..

CLOSING ON
Tommy Keahbone

Closing on
to things lost.
past journey
illusion
wisps of smoke
blown by the wind
scattered
across time.
Mirrored waters
reflecting images
ripples
cleansing anew.
Washed,
forming image,
shimmering,
distorted.
Mournful rain
tears
We've come far
you
I.

OTHER WORLDS
Garth Lahren

I dream, and I am another world
I recognize them not as this
world but possibly a different
one every night...
Much the same
My foot falls asleep, numb
to touch it is to realize
it is no longer mine
for the time being-
I rest...

Hair, the word means so
so shampoo it once a day
light, the word means stop.
Green as the slippery rock
beneath my foot hands me
to the water in one dry
heave, the word means wet
wavy in color, the rock turns
red, above my hands reach a yucca plant.

Pull, the word means sheet
shivers my body on water
bed, the word means light
coming in a cavern, in ceilings
conversations in walls.
Cat people play golf in costumes
with tails. Balls are rocks, wrapped
amongst rawhide. A trail...

Two the word means fish
spawn beneath my feet forever
I can breathe under water.
Dark, the word means fetal
my soles and hands meet
flesh, the word means hungry
eight, the word means time, to get up...

COCKTAILS WITH THE MEDICINE MAN

Garth Lahren

I look in the pantry basket and
in the middle, I hear a shovel scrape cement in the summer
    time.
Similar, to me throwing a mix of cat hair and a couch
I slouch in all year long. Into a leather cradle
amongst the pow wow music of seventy-four. Feathers found
from 1990, blacks, reds, yellows all the way up to the shin's
    white hairs.
A cry, a drum, a firecracker on the fourth of July. A scalloped
potato, all thrown upon mother's calf
behind her shin.

I go to refuge on docks, ports with bubbly brew around and
scamper like cats now and then...
I saw two cats that night
chasing each other throughout the dock
side of the gazebo. The black one, white paws, chased the
    grey one
All equal in age, the black one riddened the grey with slobber
    sucking nipple techniques.

I slumber, a man takes an eagle feather from his shirt,
    blemished
with white stars, and hands it to me...
I wrote in the mountain's trees on that morning
"I want to believe, she has the power she says she has
the power of twelve slices of pie or
lifetimes she says we all relive..."
I walk where there are stairs, very precise, in which
one is left and one is right. The steps are confined but both
    feet
fit both.
I wandered to motivate my next step to the upcoming view
that still

floats behind.
Although the fourth direction stays
invisible except to touch, much expression longs for a fifth
But I do know to keep walking...

P.O.W.'s

Garth Lahren

My arms could jump no longer off
this pedestal. Ropes so strong
behind my back, dropping
my weight on the floor, while
the rope's dust erupts
in an explosion of dislocation.
My left eye closes...

On the barbed wire a hair floats
twisting like mother's necklace
I twirled with fingers, glowing
bones in purple or black, lights
like litmus bubbles or water
crashing on a pumping temple.
My eye quivers in thought...

It's surprising that flags hung
flurry to memories beside squeaky
desks of thirty students, reciting
oaths to their assigned country.
I chuckle at it all and naked
The chairs disappear, underneath
I fall with popping sockets.
My right eye closes...

AM i GOD?

Joe Munoz

Am i God?
Butterflies
Single sheet
Foxes
Modular
Ducks
Triangles
Does God fold paper?
With squares
And compounds
I am God.

CALOR HELADO

Joe Munoz

Orange sherbet sunset
Green triangles
White balloons
Leisurely trudging upward
It's kind of cold...you know

Did you see it?

What an immense stage
This sphere has
For the "Greatest Show in the Universe"
Too bad its cancelled
Due to fog

Maybe you'll see the show

Lots of stars
Behind that
Sometimes transparent
Sometimes translucent
Curtain

Do you ever notice
Those retreating
Tangerine cream swirls of day?
La luna
In the glacial atmosphere?

It's the same sky you know

Summer winter
carrying the evening sky
Along with photos
And surmises of you

You did see the show

101

ANCIENT WINDS WHISPER
Ruth Mustus

Ancient winds whisper
ghosts you might hear
if your eyes are attentive

Father Sun makes his journey
eternally, nourishing with light
Sacred mother offers her breast
And responds in green
turquoise sky and emerald leaves
under a blessing gift of moisture
perhaps one spirit's tears.
Rainbows dance the millennium
dazzling, challenging death
a million points of light
cleansing birth
reflection of our past,
Life begins anew
daybreak star casts its glow
from the east
the red man responds
to the east
his children's children remember
the seed is planted and grows
facing east.

VIN
Ruth Mustus

Standing on the road alone,
watching,
waiting,

coal black hard
eyes
glint with lost mischief
the slant could smile,
figures lost in the haze
fixed pattern shattered on the wind
child remembers shot rang out
destruction,
never me,
crystallized rage
under the blanket of depression
images meld into tomorrow
no conscious thought in coma
sharp shock falls into place
seething hostile blood
screams attention
lost in the shuffle
man child murdered
by another
who continues
on,

posing as his brother.

MISSING SECRET
Ruth Mustus

Cloaked figures, heads bowed
Little black boxes
In the middle of the night

Journey unto the light?
Secrecy, in hushed whispers
Shooken awake
To bury the grave
Punishment is spoken

Prayer at mealtime only token
Daybreak verses
Ring the bell
Light a candle
Shed no tears
Angel's mercy guiding lost souls

Ruth Mustus

My little brother was two years younger than me. Today I hated him, all we ever did was fight. He was always the first to say , "Not me" so I always got the blame.

On the reserve the north end was "our end." My uncle's house was the first one, then my granny's, my aunty's, then ours. I grew up with all the boys and we played cowboys and Indians on real horses. My uncle moved to the west-end to look after the band's farm, taking my two cousins, our gang was reduced to three. When their house was vacated, my dad's friend, a Cardinal, moved in, Porcupine and Chickey had a pretty big family, Chrissy, Mike, Derek, Jeff, Annie, Keith, Calvin and David Jr. Since my brother and I were the only siblings in our family theirs seemed big to us.

I played house and dollies with Annie all the time and we took care of Calvin. Porcupine was a friend of my dads, but when he and Chickey drank they turned mean and we'd have to hide under the bed to avoid the cross-fire.

Calvin had the curliest black hair and big brown eyes, he had a soft voice and he liked to play with me and Annie. Davey was younger, but he hung out with the boys more and liked to tease a lot. He wasn't interested in "girl stuff" and would always wreck our houses, he seemed to enjoy this and we considered him a big pest.

That summer Calvin became my "little brother." Maybe because he was so cute he was shunned by the older boys as a "sissy." We became close that summer, experiencing a lot together. My parents didn't fight like theirs did, Porkey would punch Chickey and they would threaten to shoot each other.

Some nights Calvin and Annie would sneak to our house
when it got really bad. I would bring them home sometimes
when my parents were away and give them something to eat.
Annie was also smaller than me and I would give her clothes
that I no longer fit. My mother never seemed to noticed this.
As mid-summer approached Porkey and Chickey's fighting
got worse. The kids started sleeping in bushes, then Chrissy
ran away, Chrissy took care of them usually, she was gone ,
Annie, being the only girl, had to take her place, I saw less of
her, as she was now permanent baby-sitter, maid and chief
cook.
Calvin loved to draw and we would play school, I taught him
how to write his name, and he was actually looking forward to
school in the fall. I loved being his teacher, for once I didn't
have to take orders from somebody older. He and I would
even play with my dolls, something none of the other boys I
knew would never ever do. There was a lot of bush between
our houses and a lot of ditch with tall grass, we would make
grass forts and pretend we were in the jungle. He was great at
making monkey noises. We would watch Sesame Street
together, and then pretend we could speak French, in our
secret language. We used to play in the number of old cars in
my grandmother's yard, jumping from one to the other,
playing tag. They always told us to quit playing there,
somebody'd surely crack open their head one of these days.
As the summer progressed, so did Porkeys drinking, the
fighting got worse and worse. Finally, one day a brand new
car pulled into the yard, slowly it made its way, trying
desperately to avoid the huge pot-holes. The car had no dents
or rust spots and was so quiet you could barely hear it. Us
kids stopped what we were doing and stared at the white lady
who got out. White people coming always meant trouble. She
went into the house and we could hear Chickey cussing her
out. She emerged moments later, trotting to the car at a pace
eager to leave the scene. We saw the same car pull in that
afternoon, followed by a cop car. White people always meant

trouble. Chickey called Calvin and David down from out of the trees we were hiding in, and told them they were going away with the "nice white woman" for awhile. I asked her why and she never answered me, the boys kept asking where they were going and what the cop was doing here, but Chickey just looked sad and didn't say a word.

The next time I saw Calvin, he seemed like a different person, we went swimming and he had bruises all over his neck and back, I asked him what had happened. He said he had fallen down some stairs. I knew he was lying, he didn't look at me when he talked. He was home for the weekend to visit and wouldbe returning to his foster parent's place on Sunday. The social worker told him he was better off with these people that didn't drink or fight. All he told me was they didn't seem to like Indians at all. He just wasn't the same.

I remember the day they came home, David was quiet and had a strange lost look in his eyes, as though his spirit had been broken. It probably had in the weeks that had passed since we last hung out together. A lot must have happened wherever they had gone. They had a closed casket at Calvin's funeral.

The coroner's report said the cause of death was a severe head trauma, due to multiple contusions. I guess he must have fallen down them stairs again.

Ruth Mustus

His little brother stirred, he gave the swing a gentle push with his foot and the soft creaking of the hemp rope against the rusty nail in the wall resumed. He lay on the bed staring up at the ceiling, the passing swing casting shadows as it crossed the path of the oil lamp. He could hear his grandparents arguing, they didn't live with him, they were only baby sitting, usually he felt safe with them. His grandfather was a wise man, always telling him stories and showing him how things were done in the old days. He even taught him some of his songs, he sang one to himself now, covering his ears, to muffle out the angry shouts.

His four-year-old mind tried to comprehend the entire switch in personalities going on now. His grandmother was so loving and soft spoken, with her beautiful voice she had caressed him into dreamland only hours before -- could the woman who was shouting accusations to her grandfather be the same one? His grandfather had always told him to never to hit a woman, that he was a man, and if he did, it would be like hitting his own mother, for the women were the givers of life and were to be respected. Why did he hear the slaps and shouting? It hurt his ears and heart. He started to cry, but his father had said "Wican ye eahnat", you are a man, and men dont cry, so stop it. He took a deep breath and stifled his sobs, wiping his eyes with his knuckles, then turned the pillow over. All traces of tears now gone.

His little brother let out a squawk, and Joseph stood up and looked at him, the little mouth searching, he found the plug and stuck it in his mouth, the squawking stopped, and the baby resumed sucking, trying vainly to satisfy his hunger, eventually he dozed off again.

Joseph lay in bed staring at the moving shadows created by the swing and the path of light the lamp cast, and concentrated on the rhythmic squeak, attempting to shut out the noise coming from the next room. He got out of bed and moved toward the door carefully, avoiding the spots in the wood floor that would signal a warning creak, he snuck up to the door and slowly turned the knob. He opened it only a fraction, enough so that he could see with one eye. Through the crack he saw his grandmother sitting in the armchair and his grandfather on the edge of the matching couch. It was a burgundy color, and he remembered the day the Wacheeszu man, a drinking buddy of his father's, had brought them both in the back of his pick up truck, it was only the second time he had ever seen a vehicle up close. The man was on his way to the dump and decided to stop in and see if anyone could use his furniture, at first it smelled like him, but the smell disappeared after awhile, or maybe they just got used to it. His mother had been so proud, before that they had used benches his father made out of Poplar trees, or chairs made from stumps. There was only one spring that stuck out from the couch, and his mother had put a pillow on top of it, when she wasn't home Joseph would bounce from the chair to the couch. The rest of the home made furniture had been relegated to the kitchen area, there was no partition of any sort except the big wood stove that was against the wall. The bathroom was conveniently located one hundred feet behind the house, discretely hidden behind a stand of young aspen. Joseph and his grandmother had gone to the trader's store only four sleeps before. His grandfather hunted and trapped and would send her in to bargain for him, for she had more knowledge of the 'Wacheeszu language.' It had taken them the whole day to go there and back, Joseph even got to hold the reins as his grandmother tended George, his younger brother. He felt like a man, sitting up on the wagon seat, the horses plodding along in his control. He even helped unload some of the beaver and muskrat pelts, there was even a couple of coyotes, but they didn't bring much of a price and didnt even taste that good. In town, he got to see all kinds of things, he had his first soda pop, his grandmother even bought him one to take home , he had hidden it in his secret place. Almost as soon as they arrived home, his grandfather left. He had only returned tonight, and the shouting began. Joseph saw his grandfather rise and stand in front of his grandmother with a green bottle in his hand, he was waving it in front of her and demanded that she have some. She kept insisting that she didn't want any.

"Heeya, get that away from me."

"Come on, wife you listen to me."

"Eesh, go to sleep, you're crazy now."

"You call me crazy, you beetch, you have some, or maybe I'll just pour it down your throat."

Then he grabbed her by the hair and held her head back with one hand, the other hand forced the bottle to her mouth, and she choked a bit, sputtering. The red juice escaped from both corners of her mouth, trailing down her neck and onto her blouse.

"There, you have some or I'll make you have some."

He stumbled toward the kitchen and grabbed one of his mother's tin cups, hastily pouring some of the liquid in, spilling more in the cup on the floor than in the cup.

"Na", offering it to her.

His grandmother sat with her head bowed, as if in prayer, her grey braids now hanging out from under her kerchief, which lay on the floor behind her. Her eyes were downcast, and her hand shakily reached out and accepted the cup. She took a sip and placed it on the floor. Her skirt and moccasins were both stained with the red juice, Joseph wondered if it was like soda pop, he had seen some red stuff in the store and was glad he didn't get any. His grandmother didn't say anything. When his grandfather spoke it sounded like a different person, he talked slow and sometimes didn't make any sense.

"Hey, woman, make me something to eat."

She got up, and stoked the wood stove, adding a few pieces of birchwood.

She started to heat up supper's left-overs, when he protested. "God damn useless woman, can't even make me something good to eat, I don't want no 'God damn' scraps, give that to them sons'o bitchin' dogs."

He mumbled something else under his breath, Joseph had never heard him use those 'bad' words ever before, he had also never heard his grandfather call his grandmother by her name.

"Madeline, make me some soup."

"Hauh,"

"Madeline, make me some Goddamn something to eat,"

"I am,"

"Hurry up then, I'm hungry."

She was peeling potatoes and cutting up moosemeat and throwing it into a pot.

"Is it ready yet ?"

A deep sigh, "I just started."

"Sonofabitch, You bitch, hurry up with that food."

She put the pot on the cookstove and sat back down in the armchair, she just listened to his ranting and ravings, occasionally telling him to quiet down, for the kid's sake, that he might wake them up. Joseph closed the door before they looked in his direction and crawled back in bed.

Sometime later he was awakened by a nightmare, his grandfather Louis had turned into a' Geegheen' and was eating him and his grandmother. Joseph knew that the kind, gentle man he knew was not the same one tonight. He could hear him, his voice growing louder as he cursed his grandmother some more. Once again ,Joseph opened the door a crack, all he could see was his grandfather's back, then his arm as he wound up and hit her, punching her on the side of her head. Joseph stood paralyzed, not knowing what to do, he ran out and grabbed his grandfather's leg begging him to stop, his grandfather did momentarily.

"Meetausheen, don't hit Megasheen."
"Go back to bed, go to sleep."
Joseph started to cry when he saw his grandmother's look of desperation.
"You go to bed now, or I'll spank you."

And his grandfather picked him up and threw him on the bed, slamming the door.
Joseph took his little brother and crawled under the bed, and laid there whimpering. The baby only stirred, never waking, how he wished he could sleep through the night too. The shouting escalated and it sounded like there were more than just two voices, then a frighteningly loud explosion rocked the house. And the pandemonium was silenced. A gust of wind blew and the house settled, sighing with the wind, and he heard grandfather's footsteps for the last time. He lay under the bed, his protection against the anger, for a long time, expecting the shouts and slaps to start up again. They never did, he crawled out silently, leaving his sibling under the protection of the bed. He opened the door and cautiously peeked out, his grandmother was still in the armchair. She was slumped over, and there were more red stains on her. Joseph climbed into her lap, she was getting cold, and he wanted to comfort her, so he wrapped her arms around him and rocked back and forth in her lap, singing to her. Her hair was out of her braids and it hung all around him, he couldn't see her face. That was how they found him, the next morning. He screamed when they tried to remove him.

HOBEMMA CHRONICLES : PRELUDE
Ruth Mustus

In Hobemma people get paid to have children-- special pay, Christmas bonus and cheque are all words a child learns by the age of three years, usually the parents get $1000-$2000 per child per month, at Christmas they may get up to three grand per child. Yet a lot of these kids may suffer through not getting enough to eat. The band council made a resolution, putting the oil royalties for some of the four bands children into a trust fund until they turn eighteen. Maybe the intention was good, but what happens is you get a whole bunch of kids with the attitude "I'm getting 120 grand when I turn eighteen and why should I go to school." They have no interest in continuing their education. These kids usually end up spending all their money within two years.

Canada has rather strict gun control laws, they passed a law three years ago stating you must acquire a permit prior to purchasing a firearm, they check into the background of the applicant, if they have any history with the law they will be denied, this also applied to those who already owned a firearm. There is so much money floating around Hobemma, you can get anything you want from Cocaine to Uzis. There are four bands in the area, each speak Cree, but are of different tribes, and there is a great deal of in-fighting.

It is not fair to generalize that all individuals are involved in the alcoholism, drug abuse and child neglect that goes on. But the facts do speak for themselves, Hobemma, with a population of 5000 has the highest suicide rate in Canada, competing with cities with 10 times the population.

Ruth Mustus

I walked into a split-level house , not more than two years
old. A two and a half bath, four bedroom, with den, two car
garage , wraparound sundeck, huge bay-windowed home with
cedar siding and two skylights. I thought , man, could I get
into living here. As I walked through the door way my first
impulse was to take my shoes off, I changed my mind as I
looked up the stairway. The once-periwinkle carpet now
looked as if someone had deliberately tarred it over. The
stairway was cluttered with twisted beer cans and cigarette
butts. A balled pamper lay in one corner of the porch,
opposite it a forgotten plastic baby bottle, the remaining milk
curdled into cottage cheese. There were five holes in the
Gyproc: one large one, where someone's head might have
entered and four smaller ones , perhaps where someone
else's fists may have landed. The railing for the top of the
stairway lay on its side, nails protruding. I wondered why it
hadn't been repaired, especially since it was obvious there
were children here.

I waited at the top of the stairs for my friend, I did not
know whose house this was, and did not really care to meet
the drug dealer my acquaintance had come to see. Pretty soon
a little boy came around the corner, being pursued by
another larger kid. They both stopped when they saw me and
changed directions, disappearing around the safety of the
corner. I could see his blue-jeaned pant leg, then he slowly
stuck his head out, I smiled and said "Hello," he ducked back
around the corner, the next time he showed his face I
pretended not to look. He emerged, the younger one, but
stood a safe distance away. I asked him his name and he
shied away again. After a game of Peek-a-boo he was coaxed

into coming closer.

I had been living in the city and had spiked purple hair, rings on every finger, and was into the neo-nuclear, black pseudo-punk look. Wearing a leather jacket that belonged to a biker friend and dangerously spiked black heels. A shock of black hair covered my right eye. I had on several silver chains, and my eye makeup ran up into my hairline. I must have been a sight for that res kid.

He was about four years old, and adorable, with a bad haircut and big brown eyes. He was wearing a Harley Davidson T-shirt that was way too big for him, it almost fell off his shoulders. He was only wearing one sock and I could tell by his feet that he hadn't had a bath in a while and that his toenails needed cutting. His jeans were stained in the manner of all boys, a little mud, a little grass on the knees and a little blood, but he looked like he lived in those jeans.

I reached into my purse and found a half-eaten bag of M&M peanuts, I offered them to him and he ventured closer, shyly accepting them. He pushed a lock of his greasy hair out of his eyes and I noticed it covered a bruise.

"What's your name?"

He looked straight at me, pulled his finger out of his mouth and said solemnly, "Shithead."

I was stuck in my reaction, shock and pity simultaneously, I laughed nervously.

"No, I mean your real name."

"It's Shithead," he stated matter-of-factly.

Out of the corner of my eye I saw two boys making themselves available. They were both taller than the one in front of me.

"Are you guys all brothers?"

The tallest one nodded.

I ventured into my purse again and found some Tic Tacs.

"So what are your names?"

"I'm Michael and he's Sonny."

"You want some of these?" offering the Tic tacs. They both nodded.

"What's your little brothers name?"
They looked at each other and at the same time answered
    "Shithead."
This time I did not laugh.
My friend was done his business and came back into the
room, we went down stairs and out the door. "Bye kids", I
called over my shoulder. I asked him what the kid's name
was, he didn't seem to know. I often wonder what this poor
kid will end up doing in his life, getting such a rough start.

Ruth Mustus

Darrrell Kickinghorse and Joanne Thunderchild were happy together, he was the "one" for her. They were a young couple and were in a process of getting straightened out. She was 19 and still hadn't had any children, by choice. He was the same age, and would have made it into the NHL if he hadn't started partying. He had two children, both by different women, but he still took care of them once in a while.

Joanne had become tired of the monotony of partying, she had been doing it since her sister died, when she was 14, at first she did it to fill the void left by the death of her favorite sister, Darcy, a murder-suicide victim. Then it just became second nature, the years passed by. She didn't even have any money left in the bank, and had gone through three brand new vehicles and was now on her fourth. When Darrell and her moved into his Cousin Rick's place things were O.K. Now that both of them had quit toking and wanted to quit drinking Rick wasn't so happy with them. She wanted a better life for the both of them and Darrell agreed.

She was upstairs, cleaning, eternally cleaning ash trays and beer bottles and cans, she was baby sitting again. The kids were in bed and she sat up watching T.V, now and then anxiously looking out the window, every time the headlights passed. Rick's Mona really didn't care about the mess the kids made. All she cared about was her blow. She would freak out on her kids occasionally when she had forgotten where she put it. Reducing them all to tears, then she would go out and get some more, maybe finding the stuff a couple of days later by accident, never apologizing. Rick and his friends would snuff out their cigarette butts on the carpet, knock over

beers, never attempting to clean it up and would attack the
fridge, slopping food all over the kitchen. She got so
frustrated, it seemed like she was the only one buying food in
the house, and yet Rick's friends always helped themselves,
many times leaving things out to melt or spoil. She felt sorry
for the kids, whose parents never had the money to buy what
they wanted, but were always willing to hock for coke.
Darrell had said he was only bringing Rick into town to the
liquor store. It was now after midnight, she was worried. She
had barely dozed off when she was awoken by the noisy
entrance of a boisterous bunch, all talking at the same time.
Darrell made his way towards her, she saw him lose his
balance and dreaded it--he had been drinking. As he pulled
her towards him she struggled, his lips found hers and the
taste of beer and cigarettes repulsed her. He kept pressuring
her to have "just one drink." She didn't want to and went
downstairs to bed. She fell into a restless sleep, the occasional
thud of someone , or something hitting the floor kept
interrupting her respite. Darrell stumbled in around three,
totally tanked. And mumbled the usual "Babe I love you" and
all the other things they can't say when they're sober. He
passed out, while making plans for their future together,
their wedding.
Joanne just listened and stayed still until Darrell passed out
with his arms still around her. She then gently moved his
arm and pushed him into a more comfortable position. It
took her a long time to fall back asleep, and she finally did, in
that exhaustion that comes from trying really hard to sleep.
She had also put in 12 hours of work at the truck stop that
day and was beginning to feel it. She dreamt of pleasant
things at first, then a cloud descended over her dreamland,
invading it and changing the color into black and white. She
felt stifled and the whole world became hazy, she found
herself coughing, she coughed so hard she woke herself up.
The world was hazy, and although the moonlight tried to spill
through the high basement window the room was slowly

118

being filled with thick black smoke. She could hear Rick's old lady screaming at her to wake up and all the children were crying , their voices a chorus of hysteria. Joanne reached for a light, it seemed the electricity was affected, she shook Darrell, he didnt move, she kept trying, rolling him over and over, she even slapped him, when that didn't work him she punched him. He still didn't wake him, then she wound up as hard as her small frame would allow and hit him as hard as she could, nothing. She then dragged him to the edge of the bed, hoping that by sitting him up he would awaken.

The smoke was getting hotter, it was harder to breathe, she put a scarf over her mouth and looked out the window and could see that all the children were safely out, Mona was on her knees, and screaming at Joanne to get out, Rick was helping some of his buddies, dragging them out the door. Joanne opened the door and glimpsed a wall of flames. The stairway was engulfed in flames, the only way out was the window, she coughed and closed the door. She knew it was a matter of minutes before the flames consumed the room. Once more she tried to get Darrell up, dragging him on the floor toward the window. She started to cry between gasps for air and pleading with him to wake up. When he didn't , she gently laid him on the floor, looked out the window one last time and crawled into Darrell's arms. When they found them Joannes mother insisted they be buried in separate coffins, their love's embrace broken eternally.

THE TRUSTING
Ruth Mustus

The young man moved steathily through the underbrush, his mocassined feet made no sound as he stalked the great elk. He had been on its trail all day, the elk always kept too far away for him to get in a clear shot and he had covered many miles. As he approached a clearing by Wolf lake ; he looked up to the sky, it had darkened somewhat and the leaves told him it was about to rain. A crow warned the elk of his presence, and the great creature made his departure, galloping away, much to the dismay of the young man. His new wife would be disappointed, the five point elk would have made a large hide, she desperately needed to make winter mukluks. They were'nt starving yet, but his honor was also at stake, he had so far only brought a few deer to her, the men of the village were beginning to talk.

He had built a log cabin near the stream, about a mile from his father's home. His bride had been educated by the nuns and had returned home at sixteen, she spoke of one day living like the white women, in a white-washed clap-board house, with a real floor. She hardly understood the language now, but she was so beautiful, and her mother was teaching her the ways she had lost. Her name was now Esther, he remembered as a child she was called Auhzhuneek, and even then there was something exciting about her. She sung strange songs, whiteman songs, but that didn't matter, he hid behind the outhouse when she hung up her laundry just so he could hear her sing. The outhouse had been her idea, at first he thought it was a waste of time, but now at least he had a hiding place.

Esther had never let them cut her hair, she had been punished for this, but she had also compromised and worn it in a bun, to appease the sisters. She now loved to let it hang free of braids when she was alone, and the wind softly caressed the hair over her face. She was standing near the woodpile, gathering kindling, she wanted to bake some bread, but she also wanted it to be hot for when her man returned. The nuns had also taught her how to knit and crochet. She wanted some new yarn to make Walking Bear woolen socks, she thought if she could make enough pairs, she may be able to sell a few at the trading post.

She was quite content, now, she had been afraid to return home. Wondering to whom her father had given her, she was glad Walking Bear was the one her father chose, he was only three years older. In her last letter the old man Kickinghorse was the one in contention. Her mother had made friends with the traderman's halfbreed wife, who would read and write for her mother. Through this woman her mother had learned English,to a degree. Esther was lucky she had made friends with the postmaster's daughter in Tofield, she knew that the letters the boarding school children wrote home were never sent. She had once wanted to become a nun as well, because of sister Therese, she was a kind gentle woman, who could never last in the boarding school system, she was too nice to the Indians, she was transferred after only one year. Although Walking Bear was a good man, she could not convince him to go to church with her, that was the only thing she felt she was missing. No matter how hard she tried Walking Bear did not want to have anything to do with the priest, he said his eyes lied.

Walking Bear knelt down at the edge of the lake and took a long drink, the sound of his gulping was the only thing audible, he saw a cluster of mallards gliding, not far from him. He stood up, took aim and quickly shot twice, catching one on the water and one in mid-flight. At least I'll have some duck tonight, he thought, his mouth salivating with anticipation. He made his way around and took off his deerskin shirt, jumping into the lake to retrieve the ducks. As he made his way home,it started to lightly drizzle, he kept to the shelter of the trees and hurried on, hoping to make it home before the worst of the storm.

There are those that say the thunderbirds were very angry that day and caused many a great tree to split and fall. The sky was charcoal and the wind shrieked its wickedness . The tree branches swayed nervously and groaned in protest, there were no animals to be seen. Except a nervous jackrabbit

121

who would stay in one spot only long enough to chatter a
warning, then quickly disappear into the brush.   The wind
whipped the tall grasses into a field of frenzy.   Leaves left
the safe haven of branches to be carried on. The drizzle
turned into torrential downpour, unlike any within recent
memory, the earth drank in the moisture with relish.

Each thrust of rain was punctuated by the deafening
howls of the mighty thunderbirds as they roared their
discontent. Walking Bear crawled under the protective
shelter of a low overhang of spruce boughs. He would wait
until the storm subsided. He could smell something in the air,
perhaps it was his own fear. He started to sing, offering and
praying for safe delivery home.   He was at the top of one of
the great hills that overlooked a meadow, from underneath
the boughs he could see a giant silver-tipped grizzly lumber-
ing in his direction. He crawled out, not trusting his eyes, he
rubbed them, no it was still there, and becoming nearer and
clearer. For a moment he was paralyzed, then an intense
explosion lit the entire meadow. Both he and the grizzly
looked up, a mighty shadow soared by, its eyes dazzling,
almost teasing, the massive creature turned on the bear and
in an instant a bolt of lightning struck the grizzly, one second
he was there, the next, he was nothing but a pile of ashes.

Walking Bear stood, stunned in disbelief, he of course,
knew of the legends, but could not recall when they had last
made themselves so visible, he was no longer frightened. He
watched in awe as the great bird circled the hilltop, he could
hear in the distance, the others. Once in awhile, the grandfather of all would make himself be known, as the thunder
and lightning reached heights incapable of description to
mere mortals. As the thunderbirds gathered for a final pass,
the one who had disintegrated the grizzly looked directly at
Walking Bear and swooped down, he closed his eyes, bracing
himself for whatever was to become of him. He felt a rush of
cold hard air and cautiously opened his eyes, the thunderbird hovered above and dropped his lightning-maker beside
him. Then the magnificent bird join the others.
He was magnetically drawn toward it. It seemed to have a life

122

of its own and glowed within, the thunder energy. All colors seemed to have found their origin here. He carefully wrapped it within his bundle and carried it with both hands, like a baby, nestled against his chest. He left the two ducks on the spot where the grizzly once stood. He did not know how to explain how he felt, only that he had been chosen for some great deed and that he must not fail. That the completion would be of great significance to his people, and that many would not believe him, he had to somehow overcome this. In his heart he was true.

The intense warmth of the bundle dried off his buckskin shirt, as he made his way home. As always, after rainfall, nature has cleansed itself, and the freshness of the air made him feel glad to be alive. Father Sun made his reappearance, and a huge rainbow extended over the valley, he started to sing a song his father had given him. He walked down a rabbit trail, along the hillside amidst the thousand shades of green, stopping only once to admire the gifts of the creator. It seemed to him he had never seen flowers so brilliant or felt such vibrancy in the air, and the animals he encountered expressed the same feelings.

"Good day, two legged brother."

"Greetings brother deer, its good to be alive."

"Heya."

In the distance he could see the great elk he had stalked all day, he called to it, thanking this brother for bringing him on this journey of discovery, far from home. He encountered the biggest strawberry patch he had ever seen, and he stooped over for quite some time picking some of the juiciest, plumpest berries ever. He would not go home empty-handed. On his lengthy walk home he met with every manner of creature, from the delicate little hummingbird, who hummed its pleasure in greeting, to the crusty old badger who merely mumbled, and finally a mountain lion.

"Brother mountain lion, what brings you to the valley?"

"I have been summoned by the great ones to greet you, as a friend, as it used to be, before the white two-legged ones came here."

"Greetings then, it is a good day to be alive."

"The good days are numbered my friend, the white two-leg ones tell lies to make the red two-legs believe their ways are better."

"We cannot stop them, they do not respect our gifts and think nothing of breaking promises to us."

"That is why you were chosen by the great ones, to prove their power still exists if the red ones abandon the white ways and go back to their true selves the mother will survive. The white two-legs do not respect anything but the green paper and will stop at nothing if it involves getting more of it."

"What am I to do? , brother."

"You are to show the two-legs the lightning maker, tell them the old ways must be returned, only then can we live in harmony. Tell them their grandchildren's children are depending on them. That the red two-legs are correct and the white ones are wrong, that they bring destruction and disrespect to our mother. They will rape her, and all creatures will suffer, even ones you have never seen in far off lands of the yellow and black two-legged brothers. Walk no longer in fear brother, for you are chosen."

Walking Bear blinked and the mountain lion was gone.

Dusk was approaching, the red-orange glow melding into tangerine pink which became the violet indigo of the night sky. Night creatures made their appearance early on this occasion, calling down words of encouragement, they all knew him. Fireflies lit his way home, and he could now hear the soft gurgling of a creek, he knelt down and drank. Two fish jumped onto the bank beside him, offering themselves, an owl hooted.

"Not for you silly man, but for your honor and your wife."

He thanked the spirits and the fish.

He started up again, singing at the top of his lungs, songs came out that he had never heard before, songs in other languages, the languages of the four-legs and winged-ones.

In the distance he caught the glow of light from a cabin window, his cabin window. He could see his wife, sitting beside it, she looked out, but did not see him. He entered the cabin.

Esther looked up, startled, then put down her sewing. Walking Bear offered the two fish, she stood up and set to cleaning them outside. He unwrapped the bundle, it still pulsated with power, he did not have the words to explain to her in English . So he sat on the bed he had made and had a smoke. He would see his father in the morning, and he wrapped the bundle up and put it up high, in the rafters.

She was a good cook, and within the hour he was satiated. He leaned his chair back against the wall and closed his eyes, now he was tired.

"Good food ,woman."

"They showed me how at the convent, they showed me a lot of things, I could even make you a clothes like the white men wear."

"I have some hazah--berries," he remembered outloud and he reached into his pouch, handing them to her.

"Where did you get these?" They have to be the biggest ones I have ever seen. If you show me where they are I can make preserves of them for the winter."

"Too far away, day's walk for you."

She cast her eyes downward and said nothing more. She wished she knew more words in Cree, or that he would at least make the effort to try and learn some of English. She did not question him about where he was or why it had taken him so long, only to return with two fish. She knew that she could not insult him that way. She tidied up the dishes and then made ready for bed. He joined her shortly after, falling asleep quickly, as one does when they are tired and full.

The next morning he set off at daybreak, grabbing some of the bread she had made and some leftover fish as his breakfast, she did not even stir.

Walking Bear wondered what his father would say, he was a wise man and would know what to do. When he arrived though, there was no fire burning and no one to be seen. He checked with the nearest camp.

125

" Tansai."

" Wenando."

"I have come to see my father, but he is not home."
That young wife of yours already got you asking advice from
your father? "Teased the old man Red hawk. Red Hawk was
an old friend of his father's.

"Nah, you know women, she knows who the boss is."

"I don't think you know women if that's the way you think,
he,he,he. Your father and mother have gone to visit your
mother's sister, on the other side of the lake, they will be back
in awhile, two weeks at the most."
He wanted to tell Red Hawk about what had transpired
yesterday, but something held him back, then, as if reading
his mind.

"That was some storm yesterday, I don't ever remember it
being that bad, nearly scared off all my horses. It was surely
a sign."
Heya."

"Though you'd never know it today, why don't you come
inside and have some tea?"

"I will have to do that some other time, uncle, I have to go
see my mother-in-law." What , you have to go see that
woman?, Is it that bad? Do you want to trade your young wife
in so soon? Maybe she needs a man that can handle her, like
me, I could use another wife,he,he,he."

"What? an old man like you would not be able to keep up
with her. No we have no problems like that, only that I cannot
speak to her well enough, I need her mother to teach her the
real language."

"Well, make sure you come and visit again, next time
bring your wife, what good is her youth if you cannot show it
off? he,he, he."

With that Walking Bear continued on, to his in-laws
house. There they fed him and he had some tea, talking with
his father-in-law, Winter wolf.

"Your daughter is a good woman, but I cannot speak with
her."

"I know, I am ashamed she cannot speak Cree, but her

126

mother wanted her to go to that school. There she forgot who she really is. My wife can also speak the English well enough though, maybe she could stay with you for awhile to help, it would help my ears to not hear Bright Eyes complain about not seeing her daughter enough."

Walking Bear knew what it would look like to the rest of the men, if he had his mother-in-law living with him. But he also knew that to refuse would be an insult to his father-in-law. So he accepted, but kept his secret. He felt he could only trust his father to guide him in that respect.

"Thank you father, I am grateful for your wisdom and sacrifice, I will take care of your wife as well as mine."

"You will do well to listen to all she tells you, she will not stop until she gets what she wants," he whispered to him.

When they returned, his Esthers face lit up, and she spoke non-stop to her mother for a half an hour. He spent the day chopping wood, and busying himself with small chores that would keep him around the house. He listened to the two of them and longed for the day when he could say something to her that would bring a smile to her face and her musical laughter. As the days went on, he found himself liking his mother-in-law, she was a kind woman, who was patient with him. The three of them would laugh when he made a mistake, and when Esther made a mistake in their attempt to learn each other's language.

Walking Bear found himself trusting Bright Eyes more and more, he finally gave in and told her and Esther the story of the Thunderbird. Although it had happened only three days before, it seemed a much longer time, and when he was finished he felt relieved. He did not have all the words to explain and fumbled in his speech, alternating between Cree and English. The women were amazed and excited, Bright Eyes said they should have a feast thanking the birds, immediately, and scolded him for not saying anything sooner. Esther wanted to see it. Bright Eyes then told her, she should be more concerned about preparations, and to leave things alone, that if it were meant for her, she would have gotten it.

Walking Bear went hunting the next day, for the feast they would have. Bright Eyes went home to tell her husband all that had happened. It was Sunday, Esther put on her best dress and walked the five miles to the church.

It was the kind of day that makes you glad to be alive. Crisp and clear in the early morning, with dew dancing on the edges of leaves and blades of grass. There was mist crawling around in the lower swampy areas, giving it a magical feel. It was still too cold for the flies and mosquitos and the flowers were just starting to open up. The bottom of Esthers dress caught many droplets and soon looked three shades darker than the top. A deer grazing looked up, saw her and ran, but she didn't notice. She stopped by a stream to look at herself and took a drink. She could smell something wonderful, but didn't know what it was, the sweetgrass was invisible to her.

An owl jumped out of a poplar tree and screeched by, scaring her, even she knew that to see one this early was pretty rare. For some reason she thought she should go back, but she was almost there. It didn't take her long to arrive at a cousin's cabin, and when she got there, she forgot the feeling of uneasiness that had come upon her only momentarily. Her cousin was also a residential school product and was getting ready for the services, they set out from there together.

They sang all the hymns by heart, and Father Damian thanked them for attending, saying that they had the best voices and he wished he could sing as well as they did.

Esther waited until everyone had gone, sitting in the shade at the side of the clapboard building. She went to the priests back entrance and knocked on the door.
Father looked quite different without his garb. He was young, and ambitious, this was his first parish assignment.

He was tall and blond with green eyes, he was only 20 years old. He had made up his mind that he was going to impress his superiors into a transfer as soon as possible. He liked Indians, was fascinated by their culture and had even considered a career in ethnology or anthropology. He knew

128

that there was more money to be had elsewhere, and he didn't like being cloistered up in the middle of nowhere, now if he could get assigned to the Amazon or Africa, there he could be excited, they were always finding something there. While he was preparing for the two day trip back to town his thoughts were interrupted by a soft knock at the door. He opened it and there stood Esther, he had thought she was one of the most beautiful woman he had ever seen, he was entranced by her skin tone, her shiny black hair, her deep brown eyes and full red lips.

"Hello, can I help you my daughter?" he felt foolish calling her his daughter.

"Yes, father, may I have a word with you?"

He was impressed at how well she spoke English.

"By all means, have a seat," he knew he shouldn't be talking to her here, in his private chambers, they should be outside, where others would see them.

"What brings you to me, my child?"

"I have something, well, my husband found it, I thought maybe you could explain to me what it means. I have only just returned here, I too was going to marry Christ and now I am questioning, I am confused."

"The lord is so diverse that it is not wrong to question, he will eventually reveal to you that which you seek , you must be patient, tell me what bothers you."

Esther took out the deerskin bundle and placed it on his desk. She opened it up and there it lay, it was glowing an angry red. When she first found it , it seemed a cool blue, then she saw it change to green, still it had the energy, drawing her to it. She explained to the priest how the Thunderbird had given it to Walking Bear, how could God do this sort of thing, something was supposed to be only a legend? What if her mother and husband were right, that the red ways were best.

"The lord works in mysterious ways. He is testing your faith, my child. You are doing the right thing. Let me take this burden from you and I will ask the bishop." Father Damian was amazed at the power he could feel in the bundle, he had never been so excited in his entire life, but he must not let her know.

"I will have an answer for you next week my child, come back then."

"Thank you so much, Father, I am so glad you understand these things."

Esther felt good on the way home, she sang and skipped along, running, sometimes stumbling and laughing.

When she arrived, her father, mother and husband all sat outside waiting for her, they did not look happy. Her father spoke sternly to her in Cree.

"What have you done with the bundle?"

She felt like she was a child again, but she answered in a strong voice.

"I have given it to Father Damian, who thinks its so important he is going to the Bishop."

"You stupid girl, it is too important to be in the hands of a white man. I don't know why you had to go to that school, they are wrong and now we suffer because you have no respect for the ways of our ancestors, you have ruined everything." She looked to Walking Bear for sympathy, he only gave her a hard, cold stare in return. Even her mother had harsh words for her.

"How is your husband to trust you now, that you steal from him, taking things that do not belong to you. We told you of how the great ones had chosen him, instead you shame him this way."

She went inside the cabin.

The following Sunday she went to church early, hoping to speak to the priest before mass. She saw the horse-drawn buggy coming up the dirt road, from a distance, she hadprayed to get the bundle back and restore peace in her family. Walking Bear didn't even try to talk to her anymore, he came to bed only after she had fallen asleep. She waited, the buggy went to the back of the church, she followed.

"Hello, Father" to the back of the man climbing down from the buggy.

130

"Good day, my child."

It was not Father Damian.

"Where is Father Damian?"

"He has been called to do God's work elsewhere. Where?"

"He is on his way to South America."

He has something of mine that I want returned. How do I get in touch with him?"

"Are you Esther ?"

"Yes,"

"I have a letter from Father Damian for you, you can read?"

"Yes,"

She did not go to church that day, or ever again.

The letter from Father Damian said he was sorry he couldn't give her the cheque in person, but that the Archbishop himself had invited him to serve in the Amazonian jungle. He could not turn it down. The cheque, in her name was for $50--more money than anyone around the lake had ever seen, it was a fortune. She recalled reading in a paper years later about the lightning-maker, that the priest had gotten a hundred times that amount for it from some museum. When she returned home, after cashing some of the cheque; she would have to wait for the biggest portion, when the trader had more cash on hand. She explained it as best she could to Walking Bear, he listened stonily, then got up and left.

Walking Bear then discovered alcohol with his new found fortune and drank up the entire sum, only coming to Esther's bed when he was totally inebriated. She never had anychildren and he was never the same. Father Damian became Dr. Anderson and was paid handsomely for his 'discoveries .'

SHIMMERING SANDS
Sandi Nakai

Shimmering sands,
Spiraling into darkness,
Water glistening vaguely,
in the distance,
Where are the sounds
Of seagulls?
They sense the sound,
The sound of quiet darkness,
The moon up above,
Alone,
Giving a mesmerizing light,
Creating unique images,
wherever she goes.

MECHANICAL IN THOUGHT

Sandi Nakai

Mechanical in thought,
Their voices are distant,
I am immune,
Tired to the world,
Too many complaints,
Never enough corrections,
Sick of the music,
Will I ever get the steps?
My patience drained,

Fading out,
Their voices
No longer there,
Finally at peace,
Coldness in a dark place
replaced by warmth,
Oozing out of every pore,
Fighting to reach a climax,
Enough aggravation,
Just for a moment,
Always.

THE ABANDONED WOMAN

Melissa Pope   For My Grandmother, Hatti Thomas

My Grandmother
The Abandoned Woman
The fatherless child
Of an ashamed woman
Give it away
And be saved
My Grandmother
The Abandoned Woman
Six children with that man
The man that left them.
You still find a reason to be grateful
You still find a reason to wake up in the morning.
My Grandmother
The Abandoned Woman
She screams of her pain
She screams obscenities
She doesn't know those children
Those children that left her
In a home to be nursed.
My Grandmother
The Abandoned Woman
She talks of people in the spirit world
She cries out for help
She is never heard
She wants to leave this place.
My Grandmother
The Abandoned Woman
She knows much truth
She gets nq respect
She doesn't know I'm 2,000 miles away
writing about her life.
My Grandmother
The Abandoned Woman

She doesn't know I love her
She doesn't remember her campfire stories
She knows her pain
She knows pain
She knows
My sacred Grandmother
My wise Grandmother
My strong Grandmother
My knowing Grandmother
She can speak for herself.

MY SKIN IS WHITE
Melissa Pope

My heart
Has long hidden pain
Of masks
Worn by a young girls
Truth lived
But only half alive
White
Over
Red
Red
Over
White
Moments of understanding
Caused my passion
And discontent
For my breath
Of life.
My throat
Holds many unspoken words
Of truth
Afraid to be heard.
The gifts of wisdom
My mother gives
Are also one
With the gifts never received
In her absence.
With my father
I look at both sides
With compassion
And my white friends
Think I am mystical
And wise

But I know nothing
Of this place,
I know of making
My own path to lead.
My skin is white
My spirit is old
It dares not speak of humility
My skin is white.

THE HONEST GIRL

Melissa Pope

For Jennifer Dicason

I miss her
The honest girl
That lies to herself
She is a true woman
A woman to be respected,
She will be an old woman
At the YMCA
In the shower room
So fragile and worn
Strange and wise
Solid as a stone
And I will be right beside her.

THE GREEN WITNESS
Chuck Sheppard

the green witness
under the tree in a trash can ___.
the wall solid with words
and curious what lies behind the mocking squeak ___.
violent in color the tree stands ___.
water unusually shapen ___.
oval as if it were bursting ___.
tall as if it wants to touch the sky ___.
splashy on the rock and struggle ___.
non-earthling find it as if there is a corruption
and the dragon fly is the witness ___.

THE BIRD ON EVERYBODY'S FACE
Chuck Sheppard

the bird on everybody's face
appears when one is honest ___.
I see the most beautiful blue jay
on your face ___.
she smiles ___.
her lips, her tail ___.
somebody she marks for

WE CAME DOWN FROM THE ROPE CLOUD
Chuck Sheppard

we came down from the rope cloud ___.
we touch the holy confrontation ___.
now we know the sacred named ___.
and ask for anything from our gods ___.
we ask from mothers corrupted beauty ___.
that our thought is far ahead of us ___.
to guide us ___.
to watch after us ___.
in the name of the holy kingdom ___.
let us be without columbus discoveries ___.
far beyond the thudded black noise
in the deepest virgin land ___.
let us break in the ground that our creation
start all over ___.
peacefully ___.
this war that started by invention should
never be discovered again ___.
in the sold polluted air ___.
no I live
and Wish
it
would
be followed
like
of demand.

UNSPOKEN WORDS

Maxine Smith

Wild flowers sway softly in the wind.
All is dark, there is no room for light.
Echoes of wild animals linger in the
        air,
and the smell of sweet musk force their way through
        the brush.
Much needs to be said about this place,
        but nobody dare speak.

I'M SITTING BENEATH AN OAK TREE

Maxine Smith

I'm sitting beneath an oak tree
      in the spring time, all the colorful leaves
          fall atop my head
I say to myself, "It's raining colors."
I look ahead and see a pond of water
      Where it reflects the beauty of the trees
         and all the wild animals come
            to quench their thirst.
I think of the water, and how I wish to stay here
     all of my life.
But I am startled by the faintest sound
    of a deer coming to drink.
I try not to make a sound, but as I move,
    a branch snaps underneath my feet.
The sound startles the deer, and he runs off
    not getting a drink.
I wish the deer could come back I mean him no harm.

BORN INTO THE WORLD IS A CHILD
Maxine Smith

Born into the world is a child
      that must gamble with life.

Two came together and made him one.

This child did not choose life, but rather
      dragged into it by surprise.

Will this child leave the world as he
      came into it   Crying.

I WOULD ASK YOU TO DIG INSIDE

Maxine Smith

I would ask you to dig inside
      your mind's pocket, look and see if you
      would find another world quite like ours--
      full of fears and dreary tears, but a
      glimpse of love holds us each together.
I would ask you to open your ears... Do you
      hear it... a faint sound of laughing a
      Child is born and knows of nothing.
He will soon see that this world is a dream
      and he lives among it...
I would ask you to watch this child, he will
      soon be wounded on the battle of hatred
      and he will weep tears of faith.

Maxine Smith

Two came together in harmony
    and made him one.
A time in nature when heaven
    seemed to be on earth.
Heaven has placed itself deep into my womb.
    not far from my heart
        now we are united in peace and love.
Inside, at the center, in the key position
    there you are
        I feel you
           you feel what I feel
              you know what I know...

    Time   Has   Come   To   Pass.

The hour is close at hand...
After nine long months of caring for and nourishing you
Now is the time I'll have to store up all my energy
    to bring you forth into this world
        I have waited so long...
You will be tamed by the gentle alone...
    to prepare for a new life all your own.

LITTLE DO PEOPLE KNOW THAT DREAMS
Maxine Smith

Little do people know that dreams
    are made of metaphor and bits of poetry.
Metaphors in dreams play with the mind
    in deep sleep.
Poetry comes when the heart is restless
    and yearns for sight.
Sometimes dreams rob you, leaving
    the same way they came in...
Almost by surprise.

I DARE NOT LOOK BACK

Maxine Smith

I dare not look back
    at the bad things
        that made my heart saddened.
Nor shall I feel the rain
    that reminds me of the hurtful words
        you have pierced my heart with...
Nor shall I hear your songs of love
    that made my heart long for you...
Come sunrise to sunset
        day after day
           hour after hour
No matter what happens to me
    I will be happy without you.

SNAKESPEAR

Carlson Vicenti   To AHC

I am the fire
the light
the darkness
the evil.
I am the sun shining bright
on dew covered flowers.

Stupidly intelligent,
I smile and strike my enemies,
throw my lover's embrace away.
kiss her to see her smile
apologize for my existence.

I am a man
no more   no less.
I cringe to see my reflection,
smile when I breathe
struggle to wake and die.

SNOW FIELDS

Carlson Vicenti

Clear sheet of paper
no travels written.
Drum beating slowly
walking man's cadence.

Story in progress
writing man scribbles.
Trees count pages
walking man left behind.

Another footstep written
crushing snow resounds.
Sky reads ending
where walking man began.

OH, SAINT MICHAEL

Carlson Vicenti

Oh St. Michael,
I can't find a car. Not Akar, the bearded whiteman with the
nappy head wrapped in a blue bath towel. The wanna be sick
that forgot his true culture after an overdose of acid at a Dead
show in Philly, Pa. Who wound up kissing the ass cheeks of
the great plastic idol, Iky Poo Poo, stolen from the Hari
Krishna's. That horrible day when all the monks across
California, by a disaster or miracle, spilled Clorox bleach in
their laundry --orange frocks and nasty habits-- and all
turned white and they took it as a holy sign. So they put
rings in their noses and wore tight black leather, moved to
San Fran, and walked hand in hand on the Wharf, ripping
farts that couldn't be heard because of heavy traffic behind.

Oh no St. Michael.
I'm looking for the smog cars, the ones that give me the
pleasure of waiting fifteen minutes to walk forty paces. The
kind I fear will bust my head open by a stroke of good luck
and bad timing. The one like Delores drives. You know her?
The coke snorting pseudo intellectual psychic healer. The
one I met in a bar. She saw my aura, and I asked her if that
was some kind of yoga bullshit. She sensed my inner anger,
so I told her to fuck off, or give me of that white hippy sexual
healing she offers Skins, because she lost her identity to
Wonderbread, and Cheerios, or was it that accident on
Cerrillos? She said having sex with Skins would take her back
four lives ago when she was a great medicine man in the
lower Bronx, where she was born behind Mario's pizzeria to
Maria, the over worked Italian girl making a delivery.

Oh no St. Michael.
I'm looking for the fast cars that have four crushing wheels
and a demonic engine, and screwed up dead drivers from all
over the world, and mental states, seeking fake Karma in the
barren facade of Santa Fe.
Do you know what I mean.

Go on now, St. Michael, drive.

Carlson Vicenti

I wake up another morning dead. I have died many times
waking to this hell called America.

RUSH HOUR. Denver CO stains the light of the rising sun.
A gray umber blanket of smog shrouds cold concrete and steel
high rises. I sit up and shake the cockleburs from my hair.
The doppler shift of an iron stampede penetrates my ears.
Wind from passing cars rustle the gray exhaust singed
grasses. A constant hum in my brain confuses me into
thinking I am alive. I strain to breathe in an unhealthy dose
of gases and toxins. Light reflects abalone shell colors off of
oil spilled into a creek of earth's milk. The water smells of
gasoline and oil, fumes from the anuses of the steel horses fill
my nostrils. I gather my backpack and climb to the road, and
lean my home against the guard rail. There I sit , to extend
my thumb for hours until it is numb.

The sun rises and the red and white blur of lights begins
to end. The black veil which hides the truth of my
surroundings is removed. Broken colored glass bottles
sparkle like diminished stars. Trash collects by the guard rail
posts. A morbid black and gray factory spews out monstrous
ghostly images that gather and disappear into the smog.
White steam rhythmically puffs and hisses -- the eager
panting of industry and destruction. The air is thick and
gaseous. Horses scream past on the highway paved over the
bones of my ancestors. The town awakens to babies born,
people dying.   Distant pile drivers pound and echo in my
thoughts. Work men --spitting tobacco, telling crude racial
jokes-- pass gas and go about making a living for parricidal
immigrant American families.

I am without luck --nobody dare pick up a hitch-hiker in
Denver-- so I roll up a smoke. From cracks in the road, the
sun's heat causes tar to seep out. Tar is the leading cause of
lung cancer in the world, and it is justice for the millions of
native people that have died because of imported diseases. I

finish my prayers and offer the cigarette to the water, it floats and smolders. My creator pities me and I get a ride from a Chicano man going to Boulder. He has to go downtown first, I don't mind as long as I get out of this city.

In the depths of the pit, pale zombies slither the streets aimlessly. Ugly wretched mutants, inbred, low life, city folk clutter, mirrored glass canyons built a mile high, and roads like Sheridan, Alameda and Broadway extend like spiders legs endlessly engulfing the earth. I am afraid lifeless eyes will fall out of dry withering skulls and chase away and destroy the life I hide within me.

A dehumanized drunk Indian man stands on a street corner. His tattered sweaty dusty denim jacket hides a gangrene-colored bottle of T-bird from the police that serve and protect him from nothing. Stains of blood and vomit cover his pants. his hollow eyes glisten red. His skeleton protrudes beneath clinging deathly cirrhotic yellow skin. He is the product of the Machiavellian gifts of America: small pox infested blankets, the biological warfare of the past; Christianity's propaganda, savior of the dead, the infection and crucifixion of native spirituality; materialistic concepts - rich and poor, success and failure-- that induce illnesses like greed, jealousy, envy. He is a wounded warrior, slipping from reality, escaping the nightmare to be another casualty of the final weapon of civilization. It is a weapon that kills women and children, takes away his desire to live and fight to retain his true identity and believe what is right. Society uses the weapon to create stereotypes and misconceptions that cause disgust and hatred of Indian people that help to deceive and manipulate Americans into justifying the injustice of broken treaties and genocide. Alcohol is the final ingredient added by this society to ensure Indians boil in a melting pot of poverty, oppression, religious and racial prejudices. It is their secret weapon to hide their lies and insure the greedy manifestation of their destiny.

I see a fat pink sweaty white man, stuffed into a turquoise doubleknit polyester, orange and brown paisley shirt, and white vinyl shoes, righteously spitting out evangelical quotes from the Bible, handing out pamphlets, and collecting change in a cigar box. His bright clothes, obnoxious preaching and the group of confused unearthly faces gathered around him nauseates me. They expect god's forgiveness after their ancestors tortured and killed their savior. It is easy to see by looking around at the state of man and planet --just watch Oprah, Geraldo, and Sally Raphael-- that Jesus doesn't listen to their prayers.

The light changes and hundreds of singly-occupied cars pack four lanes, creeping forward adding to our suffocation -- Henry Ford's curse. We stop at a check cashing store on Colfax and the Chicano man runs in. He finishes his business and we head toward Boulder. He doesn't speak English well so we do not talk. On the horizon near the highway in the air, dark smoke billows. Fire engines are stuck in traffic, their sirens screaming and yelping and a fire burns on water. I cough up blood as an omen of my actions. I reach up and pull my eyelids closed and blood pours from my eyes. I can no longer see, just red. I hide my face from the man and watch the landscape pass.

Thousands of branchless dry oil treated trees line the highways and roads holding up voices on wire. Trees are not alive in this world. They make paper to fill minds with words. The spoken word no longer has meaning because the spirit of life is, now, meaningless. Traditions and legends are called myths and fables because believing in life has to be prayed for through books. The ancestors watching over the passage thru life are called ghosts and feared. They are overlooked and ignored, never prayed to for strength and guidance. Paper wipes the shit of society and collects

154

unseen in contagious landfills --dust under the carpet. It is pressed and hammered into prefab houses, the coffins of the living dead.

In the city the coffins are stacked one on top of another, 24 levels high, each one another story. Apartments are not apart, but are meant to house experiments in overpopulation and close confinement. Thousands of squirming rats, frustrated, eating each other, going crazy together, and the insanity gets worse, because masculinity is a large family and sexual prowess. Family is not the fruit growing on the tree that gives life, shelter, and shade when the heat of life's struggle torments one's thoughts. Instead of pity, adoption -- caring for your second half so much that life long commitment is not a ball and chain, but an honor-- men race to infect every inch of earth with the seeds of their image, watching unscrupulously as the planet is swallowed.

Rust -covered cars and machines scattered and abandoned, collected in grave yards for salvation. The smell of horse manure is too putrid to bear, so Detroit must produce two million cars a year. Man's need for immediate travel is more important than enjoying each foot step, and adventure has to come in doses that overwhelm the senses until you cannot appreciate the beauty of small wildflowers, the smell of clover, and the sound of the wind and the grass dancing.

It is better that obesity and lung cancer cause suffering, because breathing and walking a mile, or more is far too strenuous to endure, and makes no sense when life is governed by a machine that marks the passing of your life in a monotonous tic toc. The heart beats of mother earth and your body are no longer sacred. They are just more facts of medical science and geology.

Waiting for crops to grow and a pot to boil doesn't incite prayers for patience, but brings on images of big mac's, the colonel, and a pirate fisherman who steals your health and money.

The money that drowns what there is to be grateful for in life --for possessions are, now, far more important than lives. Getting from point A to point B in luxury, listening to CDs , cassettes, and LPs, watching images floating on waves, broadcast for your enjoyment, flying to the moon, having a weapon to insure our destruction, are more important than the journey, singing aloud, watching clouds and stars, praying to the moon's spirit for help and comfort when you are alone, and feeding the world in peace. The planet is dying; crazy people are killing it. These people want the planet dead like themselves.

When we get to Boulder, he lets me off at Pearl Street Mall. It is early afternoon and people are returning from lunch. Yuppies and Hippies share the same sidewalk. but never look each other in the face, because the Yuppies don't want to see their 1960's reflections. They don't want to admit to selling out for Volvo's, Condo's, and winter vacations in Cancun. They polish their shoes, cut their hair, and can't go anywhere without their American Express. They are so phoney because they have the same lost culture as the hippies; just turn on the radio to K R O C and they will both tap their feet and break into song. The closet Deadheads reveal themselves once they hear incorrect recording dates to songs; to them it's like making the wrong reference to a quote in the Bible. In one hundred years the Bible and the national anthem will have to be rewritten to include Jerry Garcia, Led Zeppelin, and the Stones.

I see a young couple; they have crazy his and hers haircuts. They look like Moe and Larry from the Three Stooges. She looks like Moe and he looks like Larry. They're both wearing nothing but black, hair dyed black, faces waxen,

156

translucent like stale mayonaise, then powdered white. It's around ninty five degrees, and they're wearing black. They can't be seen in regular clothes because their friends might see them and crucify them. Their lives are as simple as that. Curious, I watch them walk down the street and they walk up to a group of little Hitlers. Razor stubbled heads resembling decency, hiding white supremacy, racial discrimination, and violence. I can't understand what inferior mental condition brought on their ideas that one race is superior to another.

I get tired and hungry, so I sit on a bench and pull out some tuna and crackers. Everyone that passes looks at me as though I were a Martian. My head feels like it is in a vice, causing my body to convulse in pain. I see a street bum walking around in rags asking for money. I pity him and give him an apple. He takes it, scrutinizes it, and walks on. I see him throw it in the garbage after he is far enough away from me.

A group of bald headed men dressed in orange cloth, hitting tambourines and drums, approach me, and they give me a pamphlet and tell me that my spirit is lost. I don't understand them because my spirituality is strong enough that I don't have to go door-to-door to recruit followers. I pity them that they have been brain washed to believe they have claimed their spirit. I can't take anymore of this insanity, and pick up my pack, deciding to go to Estes Park. The sun is slowly descending as I walk to the edge of town. I wait outside of Boulder, and a steady stream of cars flow past. It has been almost two hours and I am getting annoyed because people aren't picking me up. People are starting to assume all kinds of faces. Most of the trucks have old folk in them and they don't pick up hitch hikers. One old couple looks like two bleached prunes with sun glasses on, like the cover of "Tommy" by the Who except all shriveled up and white. Then I see Jed and Granny Clampet, and the wife and the farmer with the pitch fork in the painting "The American Gothic." The sedans are usually rich Texans, and the Texans take on other faces. I swear the people in the last car were Walter Mondale and Geraldine Farraro. Colorado is turning into Texas highlands, and I am glad New Mexico has so many Indians and Chicanos, because the Texans will stay away. I am totally disgusted with Texans, I get passed by them continuously. They come by in their new trucks and cars, yet they watch too much TV: Cops, Dial 911, America's Most Wanted. I become a psychokiller and I think of the lyrics to Riders on the Storm, "If you give this man a ride sweet memory will die, killer on the road." A car passes and a rat faced boy waves at me to antagonize me, and I articulate a gesture of defiance with a flick of my middle digit. A rancher pulls up in a pickup and gives me a ride. His dog sits up front, and I sit in the back. The rancher is probably afraid I'll give the dog fleas. I sit back and think. In the course of two hours, I have seen every red cheeked, boney, corn fed, wholesome American caricature painted by Norman Rockwell.

I fall asleep on the drive to Estes Park. The sun is going down when we get there. The rancher drops me off by a carnival. I walk in and look at all the lights, games and rides. Simple minded crooked barkers yell out like auctioneers about prizes that can be won --pink long necked Siamese cat dolls, Coors beer mirrors and teddy bears made in Taiwan. Bells ring for a winner at the ring toss, losing five dollars to win a gold fish that will probably end up buried at sea --flush. Horns blare as the "Space Toboggan" hits top speed, spinning round and round, rock and roll music has metal-headed teenagers lining up to ride. Sirens roar at the "Scrambler," as children's faces are scattered, coming and going. Fearful screams fall from the mouths of people upside down in the "Hammer." The smell of cotton candy, corn dogs, hamburgers, and diesel drowns the air. I buy a pink lemonade and drink it as I watch people wandering about, finding thrills in life's complex machinery.

I look down and find a 25 cent ticket. I pick it up but there isn't anything for a grown man to use it on. I finally see a sign, "Freak Show 25 Cents." I go in and I am shocked. A two headed calf floats in a yellow mixture of formaldehyde. A midget three feet tall , reads *Newsweek*. He stands up and poses for me as I walk through. I pity his little soul for having to endure this evil world, watching it from a cage. The fat lady sits in a chair with layers of flesh draping over its edges. The bearded lady walks in her compartment, heaving her bosom forward. I wonder if she is really a man with tits, and if he is the secret lover to the fat lady. I see a little boy covered in fur from head to toe, and I can't stand to see another human treated so cruelly. I run out before I puke. Outside, it is dark except for chaotic flashing lights. Hideous eyes stare from pale demonic faces, heinous laughter and un-natural noises thunder in my head, crushing my sanity. My head pounds, stomach sours, and I puke up the nightmare I live. I look up to breathe and a chubby redneck boy points his cotton candy cone at me and says, "Look mom, an Indian man. Look mom, an Indian man." She wrenches the boy's arm and drags him along, but I keep hearing him echo, "Look mom, an Indian man. Look mom, an Indian man. Look mom, an Indian, an Indian, an Indian, Indian, Indian."

WINTER NIGHT LIFE
Carlson Vicenti

Street lamp corona
edge of my universe.
Burning cold
pierces my flesh.
In silent voice of earth
I find solace.

Bright and clear
tender moon sings.
Spinning and flashing
harmonious stars rejoice.

Burning cedar on frozen breeze
clears my mind of thought.
Frost pollen collects
on petals of eyelashes.
Watching my relatives
dance in the sky.

WINTER VISIONS IN KYLE, SD. 1992

Carlson Vicenti   To AHC

Intricate snowflake dreams descend to earth
melt frozen reality.
Heart beat moves like wings of an eagle.
Winter light reflects off delicate blue lake ice.
Red breasted bird sings to forgotten friends.
Fish swim in cold liquid thoughts.
Cresent moon looks down and smiles.
Wind whispers on shaking withered leaves.
Prairie grasses dance fancy shawl above sleeping stars.
Coyote sits alone and howls in day light.
Choke cherries huddle for warmth on branches.
Children's voices flutter on the wind
Earth sleeps under a soft white blanket.
Clouds blush at the setting sun.
Foot prints walk to live with horizon.

Darkness
now put your arm around me.

DESERT RAINS

Carlson Vicenti   To AHC

Delicate blossom in the desert.
No rain visible
on the edge of a dust sea.
Little flower your spirit is immense.
Wind lifts the wings of your prayers
clouds give compassionate blessings.

Drought comes to an end
when sorrow ceases to flow.
The smell of rain
draws blissful tears to my eyes.

Smile and bring in a new day
where gentle cascading sunlight is your hair,
tender warm sky pours from your eyes
and your heart and laughter unfolds the universe.

Thunder trembles, lightning strikes,
and all that is heard
is quiet footsteps of rain.

FEAR OVERCOME
Carlson Vicenti

I pray to transcend my destiny.
Single feather spirals, from
silent blue sky sleeping.
Mountains lay motionless before me.

In my hair, I tie spotted feather.
Vision extends to the seas,
strides traverse mountains and plains,
my heartbeat echoes thunder.

Peeking from behind mother earth
full moon draws me forward.
Crimson sunset rests its hand
on my shoulder.

Each step foot trembles
earth absorbs my fear.
Together reflection and light
guide me on my journey.

STONE
Kirsten Wilson

These black rocks mold my heart into their own forgotten
    fear;
and with no love or care for words they still insist on telling
    me their story.
And I, a girl in nights wind whipped by angry trees
wanting to free their roots from rotting soil stained
with childhood games and dead animals.
I do not remember innocence ever under foot;
sometimes the flower and the swing in the porch door,
    summer;
stirs a fragrance, cooler, up against my cheek
slapping it pink and soft again.
But the pale stare returns,
the spreading threat of veins' red blood returns,
and brings the promised loss that comes from this evil hybrid
    of blood
and stone.

SUPPLIANT

Kirsten Wilson

Dry rooted stubs of finger clasp around their prayers;
the conveyor issues the devout past the Virgin of Guadalupe.
    I
    loose ground,
spinning under out retracting against the fate of gravity;
a reflex towards salvation: My chin,
veined neck following the ebb in my forehead arching out
    beyond
    the stirrings of white clouds,
white wind blown light, only to meet
the weight;
the blank dull slap of skull against concrete.
Down flat, I still squirm;
an ear bleeds. And the beetle on its back feels the sun like
    no other
Can I have a drink of water?

There is no rolling with or over just
rocking
in silence of light burning bones dry;
witness. The stream is dead so why try?
Why shove myself into space?
Space sucking me down so heavy
every last step
a cliff, a curb, a mirror;
falling
a new
who would be born twice;
knowing now how the rock crevice of hip
needles a small body, all pink cheek, out
into blind light,
utensils.

Does the nipples surpass the laying knife, fork
and spear deep

(no stanza break)

165

into your waters;
picking at your meat
stabbing you into
order: "Don't squirm in your chair!"
Until your flesh stripped raw
finds solidity in an eye
shined
white metalic anemic. Finding
reflection only in a benevolent new kitchen appliance.
Please.
The nipple buds short of the long grasp
falling.
Every last step the concrete slam against hope.

Pillows, down
pillows;
And God gave man a pillow to soften the blow,
the fall;
to help us ease into our beds
where all animals lie
alone;
swimming in the heater's dry heave of electronic burn.
Hold on to these soft white feathers.
And I squeeze one to my chest,
another soft cradles my head
letting me close my eyes to the entrance of long nights; sleep:
"I shall fear no evil."

But deep
in the night the mind searches
unleashing blind slices of light that burn the heavy black
    patch of the mind dry;
light.
And I press the sinking weight of my head against the pillow;
hold me.

                                (no stanza break)

166

And hear the blood beating back in through my ear the
    rhythm that takes me through dreams,
memory;
through pounding of bricks and the waves against the shore
    rolling
a child against the limits of its crib rolling
away from the three-pronged fork
stabbing at its tail. "Good night
Kirsten."

FAMILY PICTURES: CHICAGO 1919*

Kirsten Wilson

1

The gate has been pushed open
I can see the first porch step
The sky-blue rocker pealing itself back to wood
I can see home through the crack of the gate
He's in the photo
Two feet from the gate
The gate cracked open
He can't see anything
His broken body slammed down dead
He's dead dead and still receiving in the action of the photo
Bricks bricks
Red broken bricks
Pitching down raw bolts swing
Into his soft brown skin dirt
His thick bodied skin softens red into dirt

2
Home
You see it was home
Not the wet fishy backed mob
Not the creamy olive green skins veined pink
Pounding blood pounding Man
As twenty-six year-old metal worker
As Saul
As young man with brown leather shoes
As brown leather shoes shedding the tip of brown toe
That hoped Christmas would buy new shoes
And be snow white only after
That big toe had found
Cover please cover
Another protrusion
Lies wet

(no stanza break)

A turgid swell mawed in dirt
Searching
Not sleeping
No rest
Searching dead searching home
Seeing light in escape
Biting light
In the brown
Of the dirt

3

So so close gate open
Two more brown toes
Out and he would have been
Gate open
Fingers not yet gloved in September reach
Reach gate open push please
Crack
Who let in the camera
Mob
Police
His head digging down
Gate open
Photos who pushed the bottom who
Click
The police pose over the body
Too late
Sorry
Gate closed

4

Two more feet after two miles running running
Two miles slicing through Hedgemoore running running
Second Street Bill's house and home
Reach
Cut across the Walker's place still smells Sunday's Barbecue
Home home dogs barking behind smelling sweat
How many? seven? eight?
Home to Betty the lock
Don't trip over the bike inside behind the
Seven? eight?
Baseball crowds closer closer closer grab reach reach
Ma
Not dogs not game not game Grady
Grady the men how many?
Seven eight running running
Four more four more feet running sounds of
Balls balls pitch air smooth sucking
The gate
Two more two more feet running
The gate
Gate not balls no no not game
Bricks bricks red red bricks

5

Home
Sings
Down
Back of
Brown neck
Down
Down his teeth digging for gate in light dirt dark brick walls
    fall

Down quaking earth brick thunder arch out cold edged closer
    closer
Grab reach
The gate crack bones break skin splits spreads open
Crack tongue salt swirling red dirt biting light dirt home just
    trying to get
Crack cold dark ma open crack
The gate cold dark open mean please
Click
There is light
A flash frames five fists lost in motion down to body
The gate is cracked open
There is light
A flash frames two men in blue surveying the scene the body
The gate is shut who shut the gate who
Crack cracked home home
Just trying to get home just
Home
Who shut the gate
The gate
Who shut the open open cold dark open mean please
Open open   open   please

* 1919 was the year of the "Great race riot" in Chicago

CONTRIBUTOR'S NOTES

Heather P. Ahtone (Choctaw/Chickasaw): is a poet and playwright currently working as Director for IAIA Performance Troupe. Chickama, Kuchasha.

Phillipe Alexandre (Carib): The right and wrong of what you do is defined in the myths and rituals of a family, of a society.

Gino Antonio (Navajo): The traditional world taught me about dreams in front of me and night songs. The Western world showed me nightmares, but also, this thing called stereo. I'm taking my dreams, those night songs, and sliding it in this stereo. Im going to find the volume, turn it to 11, and RIP the knob off, because I know something got my back.

Crisosto Mark Apache (Mescalero Apache): Theres a space between the water and the air. That is my place of origin.

Milton J. Apache (Mescalero Apache): The Apaches, Levinsons, Brilliantes, Windsors, J. Primeaux, N. Begay, J. Goodman, A. Carrillo, M. Sanchez, M. Freiberg, J. Desnoyer, S. Madden. The Loves and Joys of my life. True joy lies in the hearts of the weary. FUSHION LILLIES 4!EVER!

Geraldine Barney (Navajo, of the Red House Clan): is from Tohatchi, New Mexico. The fascination with the past lives of my ancestors and the concern for the future of our youth is expressed through my poems.

Neilwood R. Begay (Diné, Water Edge Clan): Mother also taught her children, "How would we know good, if we didn't know bad." Now I say, "Red and Blue make a *Beautiful* Purple."

Molly Shackelford-Bigknife (Shawnee): is from T-town, Okla. Thanks to Mom, Dad, Bro and my Grandmas and to YOU, you know who you are, for us and Dem—The Wild One is running again but this time the road is red. You think of this as solitude, you know this as eternity.

Annissa Dressler (Paiute/Washoe): is a poet and performing artist.
A. So you want something, B. Feminist, huh? C. Everyones interpretation is correct. D. Not sure. 1. Te-Amo La Familia.

Adelle Allison Hedge Coke
(Tsalagi/Huron/French Canadian/Portuguese, etc.): Let the work stand for itself!

Jeff Kahmakoostano (Cree): painter and photographer, is a current student at the Institute of American Indian Arts.

Tommy Keahbone (Comanche):
Dedicated, totally, for the work in this world of ours.

Garth Lahren (Sioux/Ojibwa): is from North Dakota. I enjoy writing poetry in the most random of order. As for the future, I am planning to transfer my images onto screen play.

Shirley Mares: (Yakima) I love nature and I love to show what mother nature has to offer.

Da-Ka-Xeen Mehner (Part Tlingit): My work is a direct reflection of my life. I question everything and pass these questions on through my work.

Joe Muñoz (Laguna/Navajo): Hobbies: drawing, reading, painting, skating. Thanx to my mother, grandmother, and sister. Want to say "What's up," to some fools in the dorm: (they know who they are). My friends, my pals: Cyn. and Missy. And Hi! to Freda...LOVE YA!

Ruth Mustus (Assiniboine Sioux): one of the N people from Alexis, Alberta, Canada. ABAWASHTIT. ISHNEESH. I've crossed the medicine line and lived to tell about it. Real Canadian eh? Want some moosemeat--Mom send money--love and laughter to everyone. All my relations. A bluebird calls....

Sandi Nakai (Navajo): I am a dancer, and my poems, are my interpretation of physical movements, by use of words.

James Neptune (Penobscot/Passamaquoddy Maine): is a 2D/3D major.

Glen Nipshank (Cree--Slave Lake, Aberta Canada): TANSAI! Multimedia artist works in watercolor, oils, acrylics, etc. 2D major working on the 4th dimension. This year marks the beginning of my greatest creation yet--my daughter Bluebird. Works in private collections thoughout Canada--British Columbia, Alberta and Ontario. Going to take America by storm!

Melissa Pope (Ojibwa): On the 27th floor with large picture windows overlooking green hills of trees forever I wrote my last words and was kissed to death by 59 poisonous butterflies.

Chuck Sheppard (Diné - Navajo): My poems are from observing my moods, thinking far ahead into the future and capturing the true sense of delirium from nature; after all, it is easily attainable from a

Native Perspective. -- Studying 2D & Photography, I find that a natural composition is a Surreal Jester if you can think in the purest form, which is "The Sacred Form is I."

Maxine Smith (Apache/Navajo): is from Window Rock, AZ; Creative Writing Major, Poet: as a poet I like to write about the simple beauty of life in everyday living. Dance performer-Art in motion. Thanks to my family, friends, teachers, my man Roger for being the greatest happening in my life! And our expectant addition (our first baby). God Bless...Love you all!

Rose Spahan (Coastal/Interior Salish): is from Victoria, British Columbia, and has a BFA: Dreams never die, just the dreamer. My dreams returned to me in Santa Fe. I laugh with the best of them. Happy, Happy.

Carlson N. Vicenti (Jicarilla Apache/Belgian): is a writer, painter, student of mechanical engineering, and warrior (USMC 82-86).

Kirsten M. Wilson: Graduated Phi Beta Kappa from Barnard college in English Literature in 1990. Since then she has been attempting to translate her days through poetry, dance, and photography.